Winemaking from Kits

Brian Leverett

Winemaking from Kits

Prism Press

Published in Great Britain 1983 by

PRISM PRESS
Stable Court
Chalmington
Dorchester, Dorset DT2 0HB

© 1983 Brian Leverett

ISBN 0 907061 50 8 (Hardback)
ISBN 0 907061 51 6 (Paperback)

Distributed in the USA by Network Inc., P.O. Box 2246, Berkeley,
California 94702.
Distributed in Australia by Doubleday Australia Pty Ltd., 14 Mars
Road, Lane Cove, NSW 2066
Distributed in New Zealand by Roulston Greene Ltd., P.O. Box
33-850, Takapuna, Auckland 9

Printed in Great Britain by:
Purnell and Sons (Book Production) Limited, Paulton, Bristol.

Contents

Foreword

Wine sales have doubled in the last ten years, but this is only the tip of the iceberg. We are rapidly becoming a nation of winedrinkers just as much, if not more, due to home made wines as bought wines. Within the home winemaking scene two distinct types of winemakers have emerged, those who use the established country methods and those who rely entirely on the kits and cans sold in supermarkets and chainstores. What is generally not appreciated, however, is the scope that home winemaking offers. Modern winemakers have at their disposal a whole range of ingredients and equipment unknown to previous generations. Thus winemaking has changed and to those who understand wines or simply know what they like there must have been several occasions on which they felt that their efforts left something, if not a great deal, to be desired.

This book grew out of a collection of ideas directed towards making wines similar to those which may be bought. It is basically a manual for those people who have no wish to join the 'hedgerow brigade' of winemakers. Having written this book, however, I would not wish to retract one word of my previous book, *Winemaking Month by Month*, nor do I feel that winemaking from kits is an alternative approach, rather that the two books complement each other. Personally I make wine from many types of ingredients; some wines are better than others, but very few could be described as unenjoyable. I would suggest that other winemakers follow the same approach.

By way of an introduction to country wines I have included a chapter on a more modern approach with labour saving techniques which yield wines as good as any.

Winemaking products differ to such an extent that it is not possible to provide exact instructions that will yield a standard wine. Moreover, even if this could be achieved it would be impossible to find universal agreement on what constitutes the ideal wine. Winemaking is an art and will always remain so. I have attempted, as in my other books, to provide the theory behind my own approach to making wine. I hope you will find this information useful in adjusting wine to your own particular taste.

Finally I should like to stress that winemaking is fun; it is designed to improve the quality of life. The standard of wines that you drink no longer depends entirely upon your pocket, but rather on the effort you are prepared to put into making and understanding wine. To become an expert you need to experiment, and to blend, but above all to drink wine.

The effects of wine upon health are still not completely understood, but wine taken in moderation improves the appetite, stimulates conversation and makes for good fellowship. If wine does no more than help relieve the stresses of modern life then winemaking is more than justified.

ACKNOWLEDGEMENTS

I should like to acknowledge the continuing help and encouragement of Colin Spooner of Prism Press; the many members of the homebrew trade who have over the years provided me with information on their products; and all those friends with whom I spend so many happy evenings discussing and drinking wines.

BRIAN LEVERETT,
POOLE, DORSET
1983

Modern Winemaking

Home winemaking, once restricted to country wines such as elderberry, apple and dandelion, has changed dramatically in the last few years. While the old country wines still remain popular, a new type of winemaker has appeared on the scene — one who wishes to copy the style of wines which he buys, enjoys on his holidays and drinks in restaurants. To him winemaking is a means to an end, it effectively raises his standard of living, but the cost does not even begin to approach that of bought wines. The new winemaker begins by simply buying a can of winemaking ingredients and following the instructions. The ever increasing sales figures of these kits testify to the general acceptance of the wines they produce. Yet with only a slight adjustment they can yield a far superior drink. The instructions provided with concentrates seldom discuss the full scope of what can be achieved and while the need for hygiene is stressed, no mention is made of the problems which may occur in winemaking, or the manner in which faulty wines may be corrected.

Literature abounds on country winemaking and although the general principles are the same for all types of wines, little mention is made of the finer points. The country winemaker tries to make a wine typical of the style of the fruit or the flower. Not so the modern winemaker, his aim is to copy a commercial wine; not for him the full flavour of the elderflower, but rather the subtle addition of a few petals to give the wine a bouquet which could be described as flowery. The pace of present-day life is such that the modern winemaker probably has far less time to spend on the activity than his predessors. He does not wish to spend his weekends gathering fruits, and above all he has no desire to be completely dependent upon the seasons. The vast majority of modern winemakers wish to use only those ingredients readily available in supermarkets. Yet it should not be forgotten that some of the oldest winemaking materials can still be used to make excellent brews, and the winemaker who completely refuses to use any of the so-called country ingredients will be missing out on some of the better wines that can be made in the home.

This book aims to bridge the gap between the country winemaker and the commercial wine drinker, to find the common ground and to use it as a basis to suggest ingredients, recipes and methods that will yield homemade wines which will stand comparison with the type of wine that the average winedrinker buys.

Fashions are changing; today it is acceptable to serve a homemade wine to guests, providing it is of a sufficiently high quality, and the vintner will be complemented on his skill. It is often preferable to take a bottle of quality homemade wine to a party rather than the ubiquitous supermarket plonk.

To be able to supplant the cheap plonks your homemade wines should possess a quality not usually obtained simply by opening a can and adding yeast. This can only be achieved by blending the ingredients skilfully and taking care in preparing the wine. But it would be untrue to suggest that homemade wines can compare with the world's greatest. Should you possess a palate that can only be satisfied with first growth clarets, then you must still have a bank balance to match. Yet if, like the majority of winedrinkers, you buy wine at the lower end of the price range with the occasional expensive bottle for special occasions then you are the person who will appreciate the quality of home produced wine. This book is written for you.

For years home winemakers, knowing their wines have been cheap to produce, have shown them scant respect, placing them in old whisky bottles and even screwed-capped lemonade containers. But wine is drunk with the eyes even before it enters the mouth and beverages served without respect will never be judged impartially. We now have at our disposal the same ingredient, grape juice, as used in commercial wine production. We have purpose-designed equipment and we have the knowledge to brew quality wines, wines which are well worth taking that little bit of extra care in making. Always bottle homemade wines in the correct type of bottle fitted with a cork, and place them in the refrigerator if necessary before serving. Surely a wine which takes weeks or months to make deserves an extra five minutes in presentation?

EQUIPMENT

The visible sign that winemaking is carried out in a home is the appearance of demijohns around the house. These are the glass containers in which the liquid is fermented; you will require one of these for every gallon of wine that you are actually making. A better quality wine is produced if you store wine in a demijohn before bottling. Once

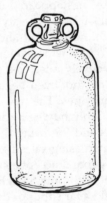

you have decided which wines you prefer to drink you will probably wish to make them in five gallon lots. As well as decreasing the amount of work that is involved, cans designed to make five gallons of wine are far cheaper *pro rata* than single gallon sizes. The ideal container for making large batches of wine is a carbuoy which can be fitted with a bung and airlock. Plastic fermentation vessels can be used, but wine should never be stored in plastic for more than three months at the most as it takes on the characteristic flavour of the polymer very quickly. If the plastic container is itself in a cardboard box, as in a sherry five, the wine may develop a cardboard-like flavour, though no-one quite understands why this happens. Sherry fives are useful for the fermentation, but you should transfer your wine to glass containers as soon as the process is complete.

As well as the container itself you will need airlocks and bungs. The design of the airlock itself is unimportant as they are all effective. The older fashioned type, however, where you can see the

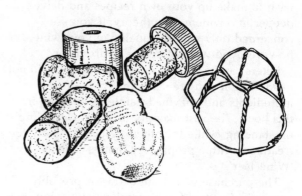

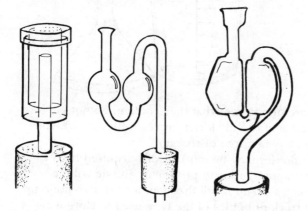

bubbles of carbon dioxide escaping, allows you to follow the progress of fermentation. You may use either corks or bungs for stopping the containers. It is probably preferable to use the cheaper corks and replace them more frequently, as bungs will begin to disintegrate with age and can taint the wine with a slight rubber-like taste. You will also need a plastic fermenting bucket with a tight fitting lid. For some reason winemakers are

reluctant to buy these, yet they are indispensable. Never use a metal bucket as the acid in the wine will leach out poison! Nor should you use a loose cover otherwise germs will enter the liquid. The bucket that you buy will need to be considerably larger than the quantity of wine that you are planning to brew as initially fermentation must be conducted in the presence of a large volume of air. Buy a two gallon bucket if you are planning to make single gallon batches; a six to seven gallon bucket should be used for five gallon batches.

You will also need a racking tube. This is the syphon used to separate the sediment of dead yeast cells and vegetable material at the bottom of the fermentation vessel from the clear wine. Today there are several designs to choose from, some incorporating a simple pumping action while others rely entirely on a syphoning technique. The cheap, easy to clean, glass and plastic tubes are very effective. Only buy a racking tube which has a guard to stop the transfer of solid material into the clear demijohns.

Hydrometers are essential if you intend to make

sparkling wines, and they are indispensable if you wish to make up your own recipes and delve deeper into winemaking theory. If you are concerned only with the quality of your wine, however, you will not need a hydrometer.

Filters can be extremely useful, but you will not need them if you are using the types of ingredients and enzyme treatments outlined in this book. The vast majority of wines clear simply on standing, while the others respond rapidly to treatment with a proprietary finings such as 'Winecleer'.

The purchase of a steam extractor probably cannot be justified for winemaking alone, but they have a multitude of uses in the kitchen as those people who have invested in one will know. They are also ideal for extracting the liquid from fruit for preparing a must. Large liquidisers are equally useful.

Another useful piece of equipment is a corking machine, and there are now some very cheap devices available. A properly corked bottle, well labelled, is essential if you hope to achieve that

professional finish to your winemaking. So, it is worth spending a few pence on some wine labels.

Most large towns now have a home brew shop. Some of the larger multiple pharmacies also have a homebrew section and there should be few problems in obtaining equipment. Local suppliers are usually enthusiasts who will happily show you their range of equipment. Some shops provide starter kits. Before buying these check them

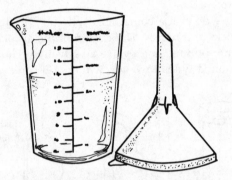

carefully to see what they contain; do not be tempted to buy, for example, bottles, which you may obtain free of charge.

Bottles may be most readily acquired from a restaurant; ask any proprietor and he will be happy to supply all that you need. Try to build up a stock of bottles of the type used to store wine similar to the style you are planning to make.

Modern winemaking is slightly more expensive than the traditional country method and this may put some people off trying a new approach. However, bear in mind that any increase in cost per gallon will be distributed over six bottles or thirty-six glasses. For no more than a few extra pence it is possible to improve the quality of your wine beyond recognition.

Ingredients and Their Use

The availability of grape juice, both pure and concentrated, is responsible for the vast improvement in quality that home winemakers are achieving. Most wines require the addition of grapes in some form; with the traditional method a quantity of either raisins or sultanas is usually included. Since about three pounds of grapes are needed to yield a pound of dried fruit this represents a relatively cheap way of purchasing the fruit. Unfortunately, it is extremely difficult to extract from dried fruit the sugars, acids and other substances necessary for winemaking. Moreover, the raisins have been baked and some of the sugars have become maderised, making it virtually impossible to prepare delicate light table wines. To overcome the problem when making a country wine it is usual to incorporate large quantities of dried fruit and prepare a fruit, flower, or vegetable wine to conceal the taste of the raisins. The modern winemaker, however, approaches the problem from the opposite direction, by providing fruit to enhance the flavour of the grapes and accentuate certain qualities characteristic of well-known styles of wine or to yield a new type of wine.

Grape Juice Concentrate

The most popular ingredient sold for winemaking is grape juice concentrate. It is available under so many different brand names that it is only possible to generalise on its preparation. Initially, however, the grapes are bought often from the same vineyards, and invariably from the same districts, where commercial wines are made. The grape juice is pressed out and the pressings are then concentrated; this is achieved by evaporation under reduced pressure. When the pressure above a liquid is lowered the boiling point is reduced, allowing the water to be evaporated off at a temperature too low to cause the chemical breakdown of the liquid.

Grapes provide the wine with sugar, body, tannin and acid, but even if these important characteristics are all present in the correct amounts the wine may still be rather boring; it needs the fragrant esters which are responsible for imparting bouquet and taste. So important are these flavourings that in most concentration processes the esters, which normally evaporate before the water, are specially condensed so that they may be returned later to the concentrated liquid. After the removal of the esters the temperature is raised to allow the water to evaporate off. The quality of the concentrate will depend to a large extent on the degree of evaporation and, of course, the standard of the grapes themselves will influence the final taste. If you are making up grape juice into wine by following the instructions on the can, without the addition of extra ingredients, then the quality of the concentrate is most important. However, if you are working to recipes that require other ingredients to influence the flavour, then the quantity, as much as the quality, of grape juice concentrated is critical. By law it is not necessary to state on the can the amount of juice evaporated. If you wish to compare the quantities provided on the various cans, however, make the liquid up to half a gallon with tap water (irrespective of the size of the can as they are all sold to make one gallon) and measure the gravity with a hydrometer making due correction for the temperature. The liquid with the highest gravity will be the one prepared from the most grape juice (assuming that the gravities of the original juices were the same). However, the strongest may not be the most cost effective; to find this out you will need to calculate the gravity obtained per pound (sterling). Since the gravities of all grape juice concentrates are measured relative to water, which has a specific gravity of 1·000, then to determine their relative cost effectiveness perform the following calculation:

Let Brand x have a gravity of 1.x and cost A£ to make a gallon of wine
Let Brand y have a gravity of 1.y and cost B£ to make a gallon of wine
Then using brand x you get x/A units of gravity for every £/\$ spent
and using brand y you get y/B units of gravity for every £/\$ spent

While this will tell you which is the better buy, it will not tell you which is the better concentrate to use for making your wine. The best for making any wine, irrespective of price, is the one which has the highest gravity. In the above calculation we are assuming that the can which provides the highest gravity is the one prepared from the greatest weight of grapes, but this is not necessarily true as some grapes contain more sugar than others; with a hydrometer you are really determining the sugar level.

As grapes ripen, the acid they contain is gradually turned into sugar. As a general rule the more sugar that there is in a grape the more sought-after it will be for wine production; thus the high sugar berries, except in a glut year, are unlikely to find their way into concentrate cans. Some fruits do not contain sufficient sugar to yield a high enough quantity of alcohol and the winemaking laws of certain countries allow the addition of extra sugar — a process termed chapitalisation. Obviously the finest quality grapes are not sold for concentrate production, but are retained to produce the top wines of the districts. Often, but not always, it is the residue of the crop that is concentrated. Nevertheless this is still of good quality and ideal for home winemaking though the acid content tends to be relatively high and the sugar low. Consequently, chapitalisation is essential in producing concentrated juices if sufficient alcohol is to be obtained. Moreover, since the acid levels tend to be high in some of the grapes, if a full gallon were to be concentrated the resultant wine would be far too astringent. Frequently, rather less than one gallon of juice is provided and the winemaker must add the sugar to make up the deficiency. While sugar and acid are both important to the quality of the wine, it is necessary for them to be present in the correct proportions and using a juice which needs large additions can result in the wine lacking body, astringency and vinosity; in short, it may lack its wine-like characteristics of bouquet and flavour.

Pure grape juice concentrate will have no additives, except possibly the preservative sulphur dioxide; this stops the juice from oxidising and producing a brown colouration in the wine. Recently pure grape juice has become readily available. While this is an excellent ingredient for winemaking, its cost makes it prohibitive to make a gallon of wine entirely from it, and if you did use it on its own chapitalisation might still be necessary and the drink could still be over acid. Yet, used in conjunction with other ingredients, it can be a useful additive in winemaking and far superior to the older method of adding raisins and sultanas.

Wine Kits

This term is used to cover a whole range of cans designed to make wine. It includes grape juice concentrates. One type of kit which is very popular is the blended kit; this often has added sugar, sometimes artificial flavourings and other ingredients designed to produce a blended wine, with a view to overcoming the problems of using pure grape juice. Some kits still require the addition of extra sugar while others do not. On the surface these kits seem to represent a better buy than the straight grape juice concentrate, but such a generalisation is dangerous. If the cans contain relatively large quantities of added sugar then this may be an expensive way of buying sugar. Some contain added sucrose, fructose and glucose, but the point about cost still stands. However, many of these blended kits make fine wines and are well worth the money; the only way to establish which kits are best is to try them out and taste the wine.

Because of these additional ingredients it is impossible to give even a rule of thumb test for blended kits such as the hydrometer provides for pure grape concentrate. The use of cheaper additives means that often blended kits are marketed much more cheaply than pure grape juice concentrates and can represent good value for money. Due to the variation of ingredients incorporated in kits, however, it is not advisable to use them in place of grape juice concentrates in the recipes suggested in this book.

During the last ten years rapid wines have become extremely popular. These are wines that are designed to be fermented and drunk within two to six weeks of the start of the first fermentation. Such kits usually come complete with yeast (sometimes, but not always, provided with other kits), nutrient, clearing agents, and chemicals for stopping the wine. Originally designed solely for the low alcohol table range, these kits are now obtainable for making dessert wines and certain aperitifs. It is impossible to generalise on the ingredients used in such kits;

some use pure grape juices, others grape juices and additives while others employ completely different fruits such as elderberry and apples. As with all winemaking products they tend to vary in quality from very good to poor, and you will have to decide on their individual merits for yourself. Instructions are given in Chapter 5 on Rapid Wines so that you may brew your own at considerable savings in cost.

Country winemaking never seems to lose its popularity in spite of the strides made in the commercial homebrew trade; it has been possible for years to buy cans which contain the juice of a particular fruit for making fruit wines. These often consist of a grape juice concentrate base to which a fruit extract has been added; extra sugar may or may not be included. A recent addition to the market has been the introduction of dried ingredients prepacked in the correct amounts to make a country wine at any time of the year regardless of the season.

While concentrated grape juice and fruit juices are sold specifically for winemaking there are many other types of food which are ideal for winemaking as additives to grape juice or used together with other ingredients.

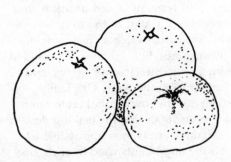

JUICES

Apple Juice

Apple juice contains a small quantity of sugar, malic acid and flavouring. Correctly fermented wines based on apple juice do not have a cidery taste, but, on the contrary, tend to have a pronounced vinosity. Do not use more than a quart (1 litre) of apple juice per gallon as the main ingredient. A single pint of apple juice can be added to either a red or white concentrate to increase both the acid and the body of the wine.

Grape Juice

Obviously this is the finest winemaking ingredient, and while it may be used as an additive to a concentrate it tends to make the wine rather expensive. About a pint of grape juice added to a gallon of wine will increase its body, acid, tannin and vinosity, while a 24 fluid ounce (0.7 litre) bottle of grape juice may be used to replace a pound of either raisins or sultanas in a traditional country wine. The resultant wine will be far better than that made by the older method. Four bottles (96 fluid ounces or 2,500 ml) of grape juice of the appropriate colour may be used in the recipes suggested here in place of a can of concentrate; the cost of three or four bottles approximates to that of a can of concentrate.

Grapefruit Juice

Grapefruit juice is probably the best ingredient for increasing, or providing all of the acidity in a wine; the characteristic citric acid flavour gives a freshness to the wine which mellows with age.

Orange Juice

The juice of an orange has been added to wines for years. Except for those made entirely from orange juice the drink does not possess its familiar flavour, rather it has a gentle fragrance adding character to an otherwise bland liquid. Orange juice is relatively high in citric acid and will help to build up the body of a wine. Do not use it with a red concentrate, however.

Pineapple Juice

Although pineapple has a very distinctive taste, it integrates well with other ingredients to increase both the fruitiness and vinosity of a wine. It has the advantage of not being too acidic. When used to produce a wine designed to be drunk while still young its slight characteristic flavour is very agreeable. Try adding one litre of pineapple juice to a can of white grape juice concentrate to make a medium sweet social wine.

Mixed Fruit Juices

There is a rule of thumb in winemaking that the greater the variety of fruit used the higher the quality of the drink. This, of course, is not always true but the modern blended fruit juices give adequate acid and a reasonable quantity of body for our purpose. The blends do not possess a flavour which will dominate and consequently any wine made from them will tend to taste rather more natural.

Canned Fruits

Canned fruits make an excellent wine additive or main ingredient. When using them remember that they have been canned in syrup; incorporate the syrup in the must and adjust the quantity of added sugar accordingly. The fruits themselves, although soft, are not a liquid and their juice must be extracted; the easiest way to do this is to crush the fruit in the bucket with a potato masher or fork, having already separated it from the syrup. During the canning process the fruit is heated; this may result in the conversion of some of the carbohydrate into pectin so if you do use canned fruits you will need to add pectic enzyme to the must.

Gooseberries

Since gooseberries have such robust acidity a 16 ounce (0.5 kilo) can may be added to virtually any concentrate to obtain a fuller wine.

Damsons

The combination of acid, tannin and strong flavour makes this the perfect additive for those who enjoy a robust red wine. The stones should be removed as soon as they separate from the fruit itself, usually after three to five days.

Peaches and Apricots

These two fruits, used together with grape juice, bestow their characteristic flavour on the wine and the resultant drink will taste less like a commercial wine. However, peach and apricot wines are enjoyable in their own right and the addition of a 16 ounce (0.5 kilo) can of either to a can of white grape juice concentrate is well worth trying. Simply mash the fruit, add the concentrate and any sugar recommended on the label.

Blackberries

Blackberries in cans are convenient to use when the fresh fruit is out of season. The tannin content is low and it makes a soft mellow red wine.

Mandarins

These may be used in the same way as peaches and apricots, but the flavour is less pronounced.

Oranges, Grapefruit

The juices are far more effective than the canned fruit.

Blackcurrants

Some well-known wines possess a flavour typical of the blackcurrant. The fruit itself has an extremely pronounced taste and should only be added in small quantities; a seven ounce can, together with its syrup, added to a one gallon must is quite sufficient. A cup full of Ribena or other blackcurrant cordial has a similar effect. When using any fruit juice in this manner always bring to the boil and simmer for 15 minutes to remove any preservative which would cause the fermentation to stop.

Alternatively you can prepare a blackcurrant wine, with twice the quantities recommended above. However, only add this amount if you are preparing a social or dessert drink as lighter wines will not have the body to carry such a pronounced flavour.

Raspberries

You may encounter a raspberry type flavour in certain red dry wines; a 7 ounce (200 gm) can will provide this flavour together with a certain amount of increased acidity, tannin and body. Whether you wish to add this particular characteristic depends solely on personal preference.

There are very few ingredients which give the correct flavour and colour for a rosé wine, but raspberries are amongst the best. Adding a 16 ounce (0.5 kilo) can of raspberries to a kit designed to make a gallon of white wine can result in one of the best rosés that it is possible to make.

Strawberries

It is possible to make a very good strawberry wine, but you will need to provide about three pounds of fruit for each gallon of drink required, making the cost of the canned ingredient prohibitive. Strawberries do not make an effective additive to either red or white concentrates.

DRIED INGREDIENTS

Country winemaking has become so popular that it is now possible to buy dried ingredients. When used in small quantities they can add a certain zest to an otherwise bland wine.

Dried Elderberries

If your red wines are flat and lack astringency, then two ounces of elderberries to the gallon will result in a far more robust wine. To get the most from dried elderberries, place them in a basin, cover with water and soak overnight. Bring just to the boil, allow to cool and pour both fruit and liquid into the bucket. With fresh elderberries, where far larger quantities are needed, use only the juice. When using the extremely small quantities of elderberries needed when they are dried the fruit should be fermented with the wine for seven days before straining.

Dried Flowers

Wild flowers are not always available at the most convenient time to pick them, so dried flowers, readily obtainable from any homebrew shop, are the perfect substitute. They will keep for a year or even longer if they are stored in a dark air-tight container in a cool dry room.

Dried flowers, of which elderflowers and orange blossoms are the two most useful, are used to develop a flowery bouquet in white wines. Add them to the wine by putting them into a small bag of tightly woven nylon and suspending this in the liquid. This should be done during the fermentation stage to avoid the necessity of treating the wine with finings once it has already cleared. Use ½ oz (12 gm) for table wines and an ounce (25 gm) for desserts. Suspend the flowers in the liquid for two to three days.

YEAST

Winemaking depends upon a living organism — yeast — to perform the most vital part of the whole operation, fermentation. The selection of the correct type of yeast and the provision of suitable conditions are two of the most important factors in the manufacture of a quality wine.

I have always advised people not to use bakers or brewer's yeast which is a species distinct from the true wine yeast. But, it is necessary to go even further — even among wine yeasts there are some that outperform others. Within a particular species it is possible to cultivate strains with certain beneficial characteristics; such yeast strains have been developed over centuries in the commercial wine trade. True wine – where the liquid has been fermented in the region where the grapes have been harvested – has undergone the most drastic changes in recent years. The traditional vinification methods handed down from one generation to the next have been replaced by the most vigorous scientific testing at all stages of production. Research programmes, often at enormous cost, have led not only to an increase in knowledge, but to a development of new techniques. A greater understanding of the role played by the various chemicals has allowed the development of appropriate yeast strains.

For centuries wine was fermented at the ambient temperature and the time taken to complete the process was dictated by the yeast itself. Faster methods of fermentation became available but the traditionalists claimed that higher temperature, fast fermentations produced wines of inferior quality. In spite of such objections, however, the New World vintners went ahead with their new ideas and today certain Californian wines are fermented at 80° F for just three days compared with the several weeks needed with the older method.

The home winemaker may not find it convenient or even wish to adopt a fast fermentation technique, but the yeasts that are best suited to this technique will still provide many advantages. For a yeast to be suitable for winemaking it must possess the following characteristics.

(a) *Rapid start*

The speed with which a yeast commences working is a measure of its vigour, at least at the start of fermentation and usually throughout its whole life. A vigorous start is essential not only to ensure that the alcohol-producing period is completed in a reasonably short period of time, but to guarantee that a blanket of carbon dioxide develops as rapidly as possible; this will protect the liquid from attack by airborne bacteria.

(b) *Stability of lees*

As fermentation progresses, yeast cells gradually begin to die, the process accelerating as the amount of sugar diminishes and the concentration of alcohol builds up. This results in the gradual development of a layer of dead vegetable material at the bottom of the demijohn. As plant tissue dies, it releases enzymes which brings about its own decomposition, a process termed autolysis.

The result of autolysis is a musty taste in the wine, so it is important that the dead yeast does not decompose to any appreciable extent before it can be removed from the liquid.

(c) *Retention and development of flavours*

While the main role of the yeast is that of the conversion of sugar into alcohol, its secondary role is also important – the development of flavour. Most of the flavour in a wine is due to esters, some of which are formed by the newly manufactured alcohol combining with the acid already present in the must. The manner in which the esters are formed will to some extent depend on the strain of yeast used. Certain yeast strains, while perfect in every other respect, will give an objectionable flavour to a wine. Some people say that it is always possible to detect wine made with a certain proprietary wine yeast. If your homemade wines suffer from a yeasty taste then change your brand!

Selection of Wine Yeasts

Unfortunately, when you go to buy a wine yeast there are no guides on the packet as to which yeast will perform most satisfactorily. Virtually all wine yeasts sold for the purpose are adequate and I would advise you to try different yeasts until you find the one most suitable for your winemaking. New yeasts are continually appearing on the market, so try them as they become available. What you are looking for in a yeast, and you will find this out only by experience, is a quick vigorous start to fermentation and a finished wine without yeasty flavours. Wine yeast may be bought as liquid cultures; these are ideal but are more expensive. Dried yeast, which is prepared by freeze drying, is also available; in this process the outer cells of the yeast are killed, forming a protective layer around the living inner cells. Such dried yeast has a finite life period which is extended by vacuum packaging in tin foil. The actual period that yeast can be stored depends upon factors such as temperature, but it is probably true to say that the storage period of such yeast can be measured in years rather than months.

Sachets of yeast are sold to make either one or five gallon batches, and, in spite of manufacturers' instructions to the contrary, it is possible to use only half a packet in a one gallon batch and store the rest of the yeast by simply folding the metal foil over. If you intend to make several batches within a short period of time, the cardboard drums of yeast represent the better buy. Less well protected than in the sachet, the yeast contained in such drums tends to have a shorter shelf life, but kept in a cool dry cupboard it should last you up to a year.

Regional Wine Yeasts

Professional winemakers jealously guard their own individual strains of yeast. It is reasoned that a regional wine can only attain its true character if the yeast strain, native to the region, is used for the fermentation – although this theory is less popular today. Regional wine yeasts, such as Bordeaux, Burgundy and Chablis, are all available, but these hold little advantage to the home winemaker. Certainly you may produce a different quality wine if you change to a yeast from a different region, but such results tend to be inconsistent; there is not one region whose yeast is generally accepted to be superior to the others for our purpose. Inevitably you will attempt to copy one style of wine and you may be tempted to use the particular yeast of the region in the hope that it does yield the type of wine you are seeking. However, yeast is only one of several factors associated with the finesse of a wine. Also important is the type of grape used, when it was harvested, the local growing conditions and the method of vinification; these will all have a more pronounced effect on the taste and aroma of the wine than the strain of yeast used. So, simply adding a Bordeaux yeast to a can of red concentrate is unlikely to upgrade it from a plonk to something which could be described as possessing a Claret style.

One exception to the rule, however, is the use of Champagne yeast. Sparkling wines differ from the other styles in that the gas is generated by fermentation in the bottle, resulting in a deposit of yeast at the bottom. It is essential that such a deposit is firm and does not become dislodged when the wine is poured. Champagne yeast forms a sediment that is far less readily disturbed than other wine yeasts and should always be used in the preparation of all forms of sparkling wine.

Conditions For Fermentation

Since the yeast is going to manufacture the wine with a little help from the vintner, it is necessary to provide it with the ideal conditions to perform its task; these are the correct temperature, nutrients and air supply.

Temperature

Fermentation does not take place to any appreciable extent below 65° F; the rate then rises dramatically with each degree rise in temperature until about 90° F when it begins to drop off again. Unfortunately, as the rate of fermentation increases so does the quantity of lees formed; breakdown of the lees, like the fermentation, is accelerated by rise in temperature. Consequently the upper limit of fermentation is not dictated by the yeast but rather the tolerance of the lees to temperature. The safe upper limit at which fermentation can be conducted is 80° F, though most winemakers will consider it more practical to ferment the liquid between 65° and 75° F (18.5°-23° C).

It is only necessary to maintain such a critical temperature if you intend to conduct the fermentation in the shortest possible period of time, and to achieve this you will need to build a fermentation cabinet with a heating source and a thermostat. Perfectly adequate results can be achieved by using a heating mantle; this is a mat containing an element that maintains the level of the temperature at the bottom of the demijohn where the yeast is active. The mantle produces a constant output and the final temperature inside the container depends to some extent on that of the room itself. However, even in an unheated room during the winter a heating mantle will provide sufficient heat to maintain a steady fermentation.

Many winemakers do not invest in either a heating mantle or a cabinet, yet still make excellent wines. For years airing cupboards have been used for this purpose and a demijohn standing by the side of a radiator or storage heater will be at a temperature acceptable to the yeast. What you must try to avoid is too great a fluctuation in temperature, as this can result in the yeast losing much of its vigour; fermentation will cease before all the sugars have been converted into alcohol, leaving you with a weak sweet liquid. During the fermentation process the yeast generates a great deal of heat and the liquid inside the average demijohn is 10° F above the surrounding temperature. To retain this heat, lag the demijohn with either a piece of blanket or newspaper.

During the summer months the temperature of fermentation seldom presents a problem. Do not place the demijohn in direct sunlight, however, as this can result in too high a temperature; light itself also causes a chemical reaction to take place in wines which results in both the reds and the whites acquiring a brownish hue.

Success will follow if you maintain a constant temperature throughout the fermentation process. Providing that this is between 65°-80° F (18.5°-27° C) the actual value will only influence the speed at which the reaction occurs.

A few hours after the yeast has been added to the must you will observe a vigorous effervescence. During this period, which is the most active in the yeast's cycle, it is breeding rapidly and will continue to do so until the maximum number of cells that the liquid can support have been produced. Under ideal conditions a cell can multiply every twenty minutes and yield 7 million new plants every twelve hours. In order to achieve this rapid reproduction, it is necessary to provide the yeast with air; so any winemaking container should never be more than three-quarters full at this stage. Once the maximum number of cells have formed the yeast will only breed in order to replace those that die and it is during this stage that the plant is at its most efficient in converting sugar to alcohol. As with most living things yeast requires oxygen, and if this is not available from the air, it extracts the oxygen found chemically in the sugar, releasing alcohol in the process. Although fermentation is quicker in the presence of air, far larger amounts of alcohol are produced for a given amount of sugar when the fermentation jar is filled virtually to the top with liquid. *Once the initial fermentation has subsided it is necessary to transfer the liquid to a demijohn and top up with tap-water.*

If you are not sure that the first stage in the yeast's cycle is complete, then delay adding the water until you are sure. Although there will be a slight decrease in the alcohol strength, even a delay of a week should not reduce the final alcohol level by 1%. If you add extra water before the vigorous ferment has subsided the water and gas froth will overflow into the airlock. A common worry is that unless you replace the excess air with water immediately the wine will become oxidised. While it is true that oxygen irreversibly taints a wine (with the exception of sherry and certain dessert wines) this is, however, extremely unlikely to occur during fermentation. As well as yielding alcohol the yeast also produces carbon dioxide, the gas responsible for the bubbles in the liquid. Carbon dioxide will neutralise the effects of any air present and protect the liquid.

Nutrients

Yeast acquires its energy from breaking down sugar, but it does require extra life-supporting nutrients. Most wine musts contain sufficient natural nutrients to allow the yeast to ferment out the available sugar; however these nutrients are released from some ingredients far too slowly to allow for a rapid fermentation. Not only can this slow up fermentation, but it places an additional strain upon the yeast. It may stop working, producing a wine which is once again low in alcohol and far too sweet. This problem occurs most noticeably in the making of high alcohol dessert wines. To avoid the danger, make sure fermentation has a rapid start and an early completion. Add a small quantity of yeast nutrient; a cheap mixture of chemical compounds that may be obtained from your local homebrew supplies. Only add the quantity of nutrient recommended on the label — usually half a teaspoon — for too much may give the wine a rather salty taste. *Fermentation seldom presents problems provided that you use a good yeast, maintain an adequate temperature and provide a nutrient.*

CLARITY

Perhaps the most common cause of complaint in country winemaking is the problem of clarity. There are two distinct causes of cloudiness in wine.

Suspended Matter

During the fermentation period all wines contain suspended matter consisting of dead yeast cells and, unless the liquid has been subjected to an ultra centrifuge or filter, small particles of fruit. Suspended matter is relatively large and easily removed. Simply leave the wine and the matter will separate from the liquid by sinking to the bottom; this method, however, sometimes takes far too long. You can clarify the wine quickly and effectively by making use of the properties that the particles possess.

On the surface of the particles are minute electrical charges. By adding a heavy material which will sink and which carries the opposite charge to that of the particles, the suspended material will be attracted by the electrical charges and transported to the bottom of the container. An alternative method of removal is to trap the particles in small sieve-like cavities of another substance which again separates easily from the liquid.

With many of the kit wines, especially those which are designed to be ready for drinking within three to six weeks, both methods of clarification are usually incorporated in the recommended procedure. The clarifiction process is started by adding bentonite at the same time as the yeast.

If you do not wish to add the various clearing agents, and they are not really necessary unless you are producing rapid wines, suspended matter can be completely removed usually within a period of two days by adding a gelatine solution after fermentation has ceased. It is important that the wine has ceased working and if there is residual sugar present you must, irrespective of whether the yeast seems inactive, chemically kill it either by the addition of sulphur dioxide and potassium sorbate or by pasteurisation. To prepare a gelatine solution take a leaf of gelatine and dissolve it by gently beating it in two cups of water in a saucepan. When it has dissolved remove the liquid from the heat. The cool solution is sufficient to treat two to three gallons of wine.

The easiest of all methods of removing suspended matter, however, is to pass the liquid through a wine filter. Again it is essential to ensure that fermentation has ceased, otherwise any carbon dioxide present may cause an air lock in the filter and stop it from functioning. Unfortunately, filters are relatively expensive; unless correctly sterilised they may also be a source of infection and some types taint the wine with a filter pulp taste.

Colloidal Matter

Colloidal particles are far smaller than suspended particles and are far more difficult to remove; none of the methods already discussed are effective on these minute pieces of solid. If your wine does not clear after treatment with finings then the problem is almost certainly due to a colloidal suspension or haze. If the haze is a result of using any of the recipes in this book then the cause is most likely to be pectin.When fruit or its juices are broken down by heat some of the carbohydrate is broken down into pectin. Pectin is the material which causes jam to set. It has the ability to disperse itself evenly without dissolving, and thus produces a haze. The only way to remove such a haze is to chemically break down the pectin to sugar which the yeast ferments out. This is done by adding pectin enzyme. Enzymes are extremely delicate chemicals of organic origin; they are destroyed by high temperatures and the presence of certain other chemicals such as alcohol. For pectic enzyme to be fully effective it must be added together with the yeast before the alcohol content develops. Where a haze remains in a finished wine, and this is most likely to occur ·if the enzyme was not added earlier, treatment with the chemical after fermentation is usually successful.

Grape juice concentrates are usually prepared in such a way — by low temperature evaporation — as to ensure that pectin does not form. No addition is required when using a kit, unless it is specifically referred to in the instructions. Where its use is recommended, you will find that the chemical is almost invariably supplied in the kit. Recipes in this book which need pectin enzyme list it in the required ingredients.

Starch presents an additional haze problem for the country winemaker; it can be extracted by adding amylase. Although starch does occur in some fruits, the problem does not generally crop up when using fruit juices.

HYGIENE

While not every recipe will appeal to all winemakers, it is unlikely that any wine made will be so offensive as to be not worth drinking. The signs of a poor wine are too much or too little flavour, over or under sweetness or an excess of acid; all too often a poor wine may be bland or uninteresting. Far commoner faults are the off flavours, not immediately identified as such and often blamed on the recipe. These result in taste and bouquets similar to cheese, a stale biscuit taste described as mouse and the more readily identifiable, but less common, vinegaring of the wine. All of these faults are due to infection of the wine by spoilage yeast or bacteria. Both types of germs are airborne and are present on most surfaces. For the individual cells to become active they require moisture, warmth, a food supply and time, all of which are present in the must or the finished wine. In addition some bacteria require oxygen, and for this reason partially filled wine bottles are particularly liable to attack.

Winemakers with years of experience tend to become rather careless over the question of hygiene if they have not had problems in the past. Certainly it is less of a nuisance to country winemakers as few bacteria or spoilage yeast can survive in an alcohol concentration in excess of 12%; the majority of the older style wines possessed a strength of 14-16% and had further inborne protection from the excess amount of sugar that was used. Sugar itself is a preservative and the higher the concentration the more effective it is. However, for the modern winemaker a figure of 12% will represent a maximum rather than a minimum level of alcohol for table wines, the style of wine most likely to be made. The far lower levels of sugar involved will further reduce the inborne protection and the subtle flavours, one of the characteristics of a light table wine, will allow the slightest sign of infection to show through. While the wine may still be drunk if off flavours are detected as soon as they begin to form, if it is kept for any period of time it will be become undrinkable and will have to be poured away. Once the first sign of infection is noted a wine may become undrinkable in one to two days. Disregard for hygiene is the most common reason for failure in home winemaking.

There are three possible sources of infection in wine: the equipment, the must itself and the finished wine if it is of low alcohol level, especially when it is stored under air.

STERILISING EQUIPMENT

Since only one piece of infected equipment can destroy a wine it is imperative that all the equipment used is sterilised. Many a bottle of wine prepared with great care, and at not a little expense, has been destroyed by being stored in an untreated bottle. Probably the best method of sterilising equipment is by using ordinary household bleach. Place all the equipment in a large container; a fermenting bucket with a tight fitting lid is ideal and is sterilised itself in the process. Add about an egg-cup full of bleach and a pint of water. Do not measure the bleach; not only is it toxic but its fumes can harm your lungs. Leave the equipment to soak in the container for about twenty to thirty minutes, then thoroughly wash it. Individual items should be rinsed six times or allowed to stand under a running tap for about a minute.

Remember: *when using bleach ensure that all equipment is thoroughly washed afterwards and do not allow any to touch the mouth or come in contact with the nose until all trace of the chemical has been removed.*

If you prefer not to use bleach a product, 'Chempro SDP', is available for sterilising all home brew equipment; this is completely effective and should be used according to the manufacturers' instructions. *Never allow either bleach or 'Chempro' to come into contact with any of the fruits or other materials that go into the must.*

An older method of sterilisation is to place all the equipment in the oven, allowing the temperature to rise to 212° F (100° C) and keep it at this heat for fifteen minutes. While this method is effective with glassware and is ideal for sterilising several bottles at one go, an alternative method must obviously be used for plastics. (Another advantage that chemical treatment has over this traditional heat method is that it also cleans the materials.) Boiling water will effectively destroy all yeast or bacteria that are harmful to wines, but should be used with great care as it will crack glass and cause distortion with some types of plastic ware. Sulphur dioxide, either in the form of Campden tablets or sodium metabisulphite, is often recommended as a sterilising agent, but it is far too weak to be effective at the concentration which is safe to use, so it should not be used to sterilise equipment.

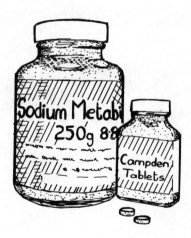

STERILISING THE MUST

The wine must, the mixture of liquids and solids, from which the wine is made is also a potential source of infections and may require treatment. However, all treatment of the must itself will in some way affect the taste of the wine; so as many materials of the must have been rendered free from infection by their method of preparation, no treatment should be applied unless it is absolutely necessary.

All food in cans for human consumption must by law be treated in such a way as to ensure that it is not a vehicle for food poisoning. In the process all the yeast and bacteria which would destroy a wine are themselves rendered harmless. So, when opened all cans and cartons may be considered germ free. There may be occasions when using grape juice concentrate or fruit juices, that all of the ingredient is not required on the day that the can is opened. If you wish to store these liquids place them in a sterilised container fitted with a lid and place in the refrigerator. It is essential that they are bottled and capped immediately as the refrigerator will not kill any germs present.

By far the greatest danger of infection in your wine is with fresh fruit, whose surfaces are invariably covered with wild yeasts. Such yeasts will, if allowed to enter the musts, take over from the wine yeast provided. Wild yeasts usually have a far lower tolerance to alcohol and yield a partly fermented drink; they also tend to be less vigorous in their activity, generating less of the carbon dioxide which protects the wine in its early stages when it is at its most vulnerable. The most effective method of destroying these yeasts and any harmful bacteria which may be present is to cover the fruit with boiling water. With most wild fruits used in winemaking there are insufficient natural sugars present to cause any pronounced charing or maderisation. Again, sulphur dioxide is advocated as a method of destroying wild yeasts; this is used in some commercial winemaking. As with apparatus, fruit is not completely sterilised by this method and it is necessary to use a starter bottle when the chemical is used. In my experience the use of sulphur dioxide at this stage in the winemaking operation has no advantages for the home producer and may complicate fermentation.

Making the Wine

The fine details of making a wine will depend upon the style that you are preparing for each will have its subtle variations, but the general techniques are applicable to all wines. All kit wines are supplied with instructions which should be followed carefully. If you are using a kit then the following methods give more details of the various steps involved.

PREPARING THE MUST

Of all the stages involved in brewing a wine there is no greater variation than that of making the must itself. The recipes in this book have been made as simple as possible; they require the minimum amount of equipment.

There are several ways in which solid winemaking materials can be liquefied; they may be macerated in a food machine or liquidiser, or the liquids can be removed by a steam extractor such as a 'Mehu-Maija'. While the cost of these items of equipment, which are by no means essential, cannot be justified for winemaking alone, if you have one then I would recommend using it for berries and other fruits with a reasonably high moisture content.

Many of the recipes in this book use only liquids. Where no solid material is used in the recipe place the must straight into the demijohn without using a fermenting bucket; there is no need for the straining stage. Using this method it is necessary to keep the total liquid to below six pints (3 litres). Generally this presents no problems, but if you are preparing a high-alcohol wine, using more than 2½ pounds (1.2 kilos) of sugar, including that present in the juices, you should incorporate only 2½ pounds in the initial must and include the rest at the topping up stage or after the first racking.

Where solid materials such as fruit or flower petals are used in a recipe it is necessary to start the wine in the fermenting bucket. Except when

making dessert wines, all the sugar can be added at this stage and the total volume can be made up to one gallon. In order to be able to make up exactly one gallon just pour eight pints of liquid into the bucket and mark the outside of the container at the one gallon point. Do not judge the quantity of liquid by the amount of water added as the solid materials do occupy a finite volume; for example two pounds of sugar occupies one pint. Cover the bucket.

Adding Bentonite (optional)

If your aim is to make the wine in the shortest possible period, then add bentonite immediately you have prepared the must. Simply add one heaped teaspoon of the white powder to the liquid.

Adding the Yeast and Enzymes

Yeast and pectic enzymes should never be added at a temperature above 75° F. Adding these materials below this temperature will not harm them in any way, but the yeast will not work until the liquid is brought up to 65°-75° F (18.5°-23.5° C). *Every effort should be made to maintain the temperature within this range until the final racking has been performed.*

INITIAL FERMENTATION

At the correct temperature modern wine yeast commences fermentation within 24 hours. The start of activity increases to a vigorous foam. If the yeast stops working within two days add a fresh sample immediately. All wines during the early stages benefit from agitation; this disperses the alcohol and carbon dioxide which would otherwise inhibit the plant's action. Where solid materials are present, daily stirring helps to bring out the flavour in the ingredients.

The length of time that the vigorous head remains will depend upon the temperature, the activity of the particular strain of yeast, the amount of sugar present and the ratio of air space to liquid. Usually this stage lasts from four to ten days. You will observe the end of this stage when the head gradually subsides. *Do not proceed to the next stage until the effervescence is reduced to a few bubbles around the side of the container.* Failure to observe this precaution will result in the liquid passing over into the airlock and possibly down the side of the container when it is topped up.

SECONDARY FERMENTATION

Where the must contains solid materials, it must be strained at the end of the initial fermentation or it will begin to decompose in a similar fashion to the lees. Strain the liquid through muslin or a straining bag into a second sterilised bucket before transferring to the demijohn. Top the liquid up to the neck of the demijohn. Should you have the slightest doubt as to whether the initial fermentation is complete or not you may top up to within two inches (5 cm) of the neck and allow the wine to remain at this level for a further week before completing the addition of water. As soon as the liquid is transferred to the demijohn fit the airlock. If the wine has been made in the demijohn from the start top up as soon as the initial fermentation has subsided.

RACKING

As the secondary fermentation proceeds a sediment of dead yeast cells — the lees — will begin to build up at the bottom of the demijohn; this must be separated and discarded from the liquid to stop decomposition. Some wines become clear within about two months; these require only one racking before they are ready for drinking. The majority of wines require two and occasionally, with the desserts, three rackings. Rather than concern yourself with the number of rackings needed perform the operations as and when required. The first racking should take place when there is a sediment ¼-⅜ inch (0.5-0.75 cm). Providing the recommended temperature range is maintained this will occur between four to eight weeks after topping up the demijohn. Thereafter rack every two to three months, or sooner if the sediment reaches the level I have mentioned. You may cease racking when the wine is completely clear.

To perform the racking operation place the demijohn containing the wine on a work bench and insert the racking tube. Suck through the end of the tube and when the liquid has started to come through place your forefinger over the end of the tube. Position the tube in a second sterilised demijohn on the floor, and allow the liquid to

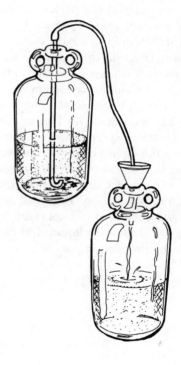

syphon into the container. Syphon off the maximum of liquid, but do not let any of the sediment enter the second demijohn. The final traces may be transferred by carefully tilting the higher demijohn, taking great care not to disturb the sediment.

After racking there will be an airspace; top this up with tap water. If you perform the racking carefully you will only lose about 5% of the volume of the liquid and extra water will not appreciably effect the quality of the wine. With dessert wines it is often necessary to feed with extra sugar to yield the maximum amount of alcohol. In order to ensure that there is sufficient room to add the sugar (which should be provided as a concentrated syrup prepared from a solution containing the equivalent of two pounds of sugar dissolved in one pint of water), estimate the quantity of syrup required and pour into the clean demijohn before racking. The small quantities of sugar that are required will not result in the loss of more than a glass of the liquid; you can drink this to check the progress of your wine!

ARRESTING FERMENTATION

When aiming for an absolutely dry wine fermentation will cease naturally while the yeast in a dessert wine, which should contain residual sugar, will stop working when the alcohol level (about 16%) kills it. To prepare a wine with a lower alcohol level and a slight residual sweetness it is necessary to kill the yeast. As the alcohol level increases so the activity of the yeast decreases, often appearing to stop altogether. In the vast majority of instances, however, the yeast is not dead but dormant; it will begin again at some stage in the future yielding a wine which is slightly sparkling and rather cloudy through the formation of new yeast cells. If there is very much sugar present the bottle may burst. To avoid the possibility of these problems occurring the activity should be stopped in all wines, other than dessert, which contain any degree of residual sweetness. This may be achieved in one of two ways:

(a) *Chemical destruction of yeast*

When you have decided that the taste of the wine is correct perform the final racking; do not worry if the wine is not clear at this stage. Then add one crushed Campden tablet, followed by one gram of potassium sorbate; instructions are given on the container on how to measure out the required amount. Always make sure that the Campden tablet is thoroughly crushed, otherwise it will dissolve only very slowly and an objectionable taste will persist for a prolonged period. Never add potassium sorbate without first providing the Campden tablet because the wine will develop a geranium-like flavour.

(b) *Pasteurisation*

Pasteurisation is the killing of a wide range of organisms by heat, with the minimum of detrimental effect on the food material. Since yeast is far more susceptible to heat than most of the germs that the method was developed to destroy, providing great care is taken not to exceed the correct temperature the yeast may be killed without any noticeable change in the character of the wine.

Alcohol boils at 172° F (78° C) and if a temperature of 150° F (65° C) is exceeded there is a danger of the wine becoming weaker. The same problem can result from prolonged heating. Theoretically, wines which have delicate bouquets could lose some of their aroma as a result of the heat treatment, but this should not happen if a tight-fitting lid is placed on the saucepan used for heating. By limiting the heating period there is also no danger of charring any sugars present which could affect the taste.

To pasteurise the wine place it in either a non-stick or stainless steel saucepan (do not use an aluminium saucepan as the acid in the wine will react with it). Include a sweet thermometer, which should be used to constantly stir the liquid, bring the temperature to 145° F (63° C) and immediately remove from the heat source, take out the thermometer and close the lid. Allow to stand for three minutes away from the heat, then immediately plunge the saucepan into a sink of iced water. When cool, bottle.

CLARIFICATION (optional)

The wine usually clarifies as a result of standing, but if you wish to accelerate the process you may add a proprietary wine finings any time after the yeast has ceased functioning or has been killed. Full details of its use will be given on the container.

SWEETENING A WINE (optional)

If your wine is not as sweet as you wish, you may add sugar syrup, providing that you have either chemically killed the yeast or it has been submitted to pasteurisation. If sugar syrup is added to a wine containing live yeast fermentation will start again.

Saccharins, which include most artificial sweeteners are non-fermentable and can be added to a wine without the danger of the liquid starting to work again. Unfortunately upon standing they tend to develop a bitter taste, so are best avoided. At least one firm incorporates a form of saccharin in their compounded must and this does not develop any objectionable tastes.

Lactose is a true sugar which is virtually non-fermentable and may be added to the wine at any stage to improve the sweetness. It is not as good as sucrose — household sugar — and relatively large quantities are required.

MATURATION

You will probably know from your experience of bought wines that some wines, such as Beaujolais Nouveau, are ready for drinking almost as soon as they are clear, while others including the clarets and sauternes continue to improve for several years. Similarly in home winemaking there is no general rule concerning how long a wine should be stored before it is drunk. Wines mature fractionally better if stored in bulk and if you possess sufficient demijohns use these in preference to bottles for long term storage. *Never pour wine straight from the demijohn* as the air that enters may contain spoilage yeats and bacteria; also the oxygen in the air will attack the wine, giving it an objectionable taste. Always bottle before serving the wine. When storing wine in a demijohn always fit an airlock and keep topped up with water; if refermentation starts there is then no danger of a burst container and the airlock will ensure that no air enters. Bottled wines should be stored on their sides to stop the corks from drying out. The ideal temperature for storing wine is 45°- 55° F (7°-13° C). While it may be difficult to maintain this temperature try to avoid keeping the liquid in a place such as a garage which is liable to violent fluctuations in temperature. Never store wine for prolonged periods in a plastic container as this usually effects the taste of the drink.

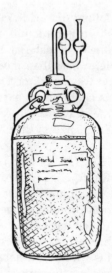

BARRELS AND OAK FLAVOURING

Many wines owe part of the characteristic taste to the oak flavourings of the barrel. If home wines are stored in one of the small barrels that are available they tend to extract too much flavouring due to the relatively large surface area compared with the small volume of liquid. If you wish to extract oak flavourings in this way it is important that you carefully sample the liquid occasionally to check that the wine is not becoming too oak-flavoured. As soon as you believe that you have the correct flavour transfer and complete the storing in glass. After using a barrel in this way immediately wash it out with tap water followed by a kettle full of boiling water. It is important that this precaution is taken for once a barrel becomes infected it is extremely difficult to render it sterile due to the many cracks in the wood.

Oak barrel flavourings may be induced artificially in a wine by the addition of 'Sinatin 17' which is an extract of oak. This compound, which is sold in a very concentrated form, develops the flavour and is ideal for those wines which require it. Add dropwise to taste, to a bottle at a time, so that if you exceed the desired amount you may always blend.

Improving Kit Wines

Wine itself covers a whole range of drinks, from the light wines with a low alcoholic content to full sweet intoxicating varieties that should be sipped like a liqueur; in between these extremes it is possible to find virtually every combination of flavour, aroma, sweetness and strength. The drinker whose taste is defined to some extent by his pocket will be limited in his choice, yet even within any particular price range there are still distinctive styles of drink. Concentrate and kit manufacturers realise that they can only provide a limited range, preferring to offer the price advantages of a standard product; they sell what they consider to be the most widely enjoyed styles of wine. Consequently, if you are not satisfied with the wine produced from any kit the first approach must be to experiment with some of the other kits available. While in general the quality of a wine will depend to a very large extent on the price, and the more expensive cost twice as much as the cheapest, you will not always solve your problem simply by buying a dearer kit. Once you have tried those available decide which best suits your palate and pocket. Then try to define what you would like to improve in the wine; the following points will help you to make those improvements.

WINE IS TOO WEAK

You can detect the presence of alcohol in a drink as the burning sensation at the back of the throat. Low strength drinks will not give this effect. To test for the quantity of spirit in wines simply suck in the air from across the top of the drink. In drawing in the air you will suck in more of the volatile alcohol than water; using this technique you can make a very approximate comparison of the strength of wines.

The wines of lowest strength are the table wines; commercial examples may contain no more than 8-10%, although clarets, burgundies and many others are usually in excess of 12%. Some of the prepared wine kits will produce wines in the 8% region and you may find these insipid if you are used to drinking a stronger wine. Increasing the alcohol content is simple; add 3½ oz (90 g) extra sugar as a syrup for each gallon (5 litres) of wine that you are making. This will raise the alcoholic strength by about 1%. You are unlikely to notice any worthwhile increase in the alcohol level, however, until you have produced an extra 2% of the spirit.

When you first start making wines you may be tempted to prepare as high an alcoholic content as possible. This is not advisable with table wines, however, because you require a beverage that is weak enough to allow you to consume reasonable quantities without ill effects; moreover, high alcohol levels demand extra body, acid and tannin to retain the balance. The lightest kit wines are often incapable of standing more than 10% alcohol. If, after treatment, you find that the previously mellow wine is now too harsh then you have increased the alcohol level too much; in future adjust the amount of added sugar accordingly. If this happens, then add sugar syrup to taste; this will save your first gallon. It will also increase the body of the wine and carry the extra alcohol — but drink the wine before it has an opportunity to referment.

At the other extreme are the dessert wines, such as the port and sherry styles. Some kits are labelled as full bodied and should be capable of holding the maximum amount of alcohol obtainable in a wine. To establish whether your kit has the total permitted sugar you will need to use a hydrometer.

Basically a hydrometer is a hollow glass tube weighted at one end so that it floats upright in a liquid. In liquids that are not very dense the instrument will almost sink, with only the top of the tube not submerged, whereas with a very dense liquid virtually all of the tube floats. The instrument is calibrated by marking the position at the top of the tube in a known low density and the position at the bottom of a known high density liquid. The scale in between is then divided equally to give the calibration. The specific gravity of water is one and should you damage the hydrometer you can always ensure that it is still functioning correctly by checking it against water.

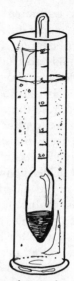

Some winemakers refer to the specific gravity not as 1.000 but as zero; this is very misleading as the gravity of table wines is often as low as 0.995 and confusion exists as to how a gravity of less than what they believe to be nought can occur. The gravity above one is due almost entirely to fermentable sugars, but as these are converted to alcohol the density of the liquid may fall below 1.000 as it is now mainly a mixture of water and alcohol and the latter, when pure, has a specific gravity of 0.880.

To use the hydrometer, place the instrument in a hydrometer pot; if this does not come with the instrument, a tall glass or vase will suffice. Give it a gentle turn and read the calibration where the stem comes to rest. You will see that the liquid appears to rise up the stem of the instrument, the correct gravity is obtained by reading the level where the surface of the liquid just meets the stem.

The hydrometer is calibrated at 60° F (16° C), you may ignore the temperature if it deviates by less than two or three degrees. For larger differences, you should add 0.001 for every 3° F (1.5° C) the temperature is above 60° F. For temperatures below this value a similar amount should be subtracted from the reading.

Two errors can result from using the hydrometer. First, if the wine is still working the carbon dioxide will give extra buoyancy making the instrument float higher giving a high result. Second, since some of the materials that will cause the instrument to rise are not fermentable, the reading although accurate may be slightly above the true sugar level. But with winemaking we do not need to be one hundred per cent accurate and remember the instrument used as a basis for levying taxes on beer works on the same principle, so it cannot be far out.

Once you have determined the gravity of the fruit juice and decided what initial gravity you require, then an addition of 5 oz sugar to the gallon (125 g per 4.5 litres) raises the gravity by 0.010. If your juices have a gravity of 1.040 and you wish to make it up to 1.120 then you will require $1.120 - 1.040 \times 5 \times 100 = 40$ oz or 2½ lbs.

It is easier and more accurate to add the sugar, as a syrup, to six pints of liquid and dilute to the gallon.

Obviously the liquid will be less dense when diluted, only 6/8th of its value in the concentrated form, so you allow for this in your calculation.

If you have six pints of a liquid of gravity 1.032 and you wish to make it up to a gallon of density 1.080 then you will require

$$1.080 - \frac{1.032 \times 6}{8} \times \frac{5}{0.010} = 28oz = 1lb\ 12oz.$$

Strength of Wines

Many winemakers like to know how much alcohol is present in their wine, and an approximate figure — many errors are involved as a result of the inefficient conversion during the aerobic fermentation stage — can be obtained by using the hydrometer. Every drop of 0.010 density units corresponds to a potential alcohol of 1.25%, so if the starting gravity was 1.120 and the finishing value was 1.000 then the percentage of alcohol is given by

$1.120 - 1.000 \times 1.25 \times 100 = 16\%$

The maximum sugar that can be fermented out is about 3½ pounds per gallon; this corresponds to a starting gravity of 1.120. You may calculate the quantity of sugar you require as follows: 5 oz of sugar per gallon raises the gravity by 0.010 degrees. If the gravity of the must = 1.090, then the additional sugar needed is $1.120 - 1.090 \times 5$ oz $= 3 \times 5 = 15$ oz.

Do not provide all of the sugar at the start of the fermentation or the liquid may suffer osmotic shock. Sugar attracts water and at concentrations above three pounds per gallon it will begin to take water from the yeast and kill it. To overcome the problem add only sufficient sugar to allow the total to reach three pounds. Since the actual quantity that you require is 3½ lbs, then ½ lb remains to be added. Provide this at the racking stage by dissolving the solid sugar in a quarter of a pint (125 ml) of water and use it to fill the extra space created after the first racking.

If you are trying to make a Madeira style wine or wish to give an instant matured effect to your wine use a quarter of a pound (125 gms) of Demerara sugar in place of a similar quantity of white at the racking stage. Certain wines, especially those made from wines growing nearer to the Equator than the temperate wine growing regions, experience a slight cooking of the sugars. This gives the wine a slight caramel taste, the familiar characteristic of Madeira type wines.

WINE LACKS ACIDITY

Lack of acidity in the wine results in a bland or insipid taste. This can be corrected in the finished wine by preparing a concentrated solution of tartaric acid and adding it to taste to individual bottles. Use tartaric in preference to citric as this is the natural acid of the grape; it gives a vinous flavour without the need to wait further for it to mature by interaction with the alcohol in the wine.

When you next make the same wine incorporate 1 pint (½ litre) carton of fresh grapefruit juice in the liquid in place of the same quantity of water. The main acid in grapefruit juice is citric acid, but if added to the mixture at the same time as the yeast it will blend with the other flavourings, giving a wine with no pronounced taste of citrus fruit. The fruit juice will also increase the body of the wine.

WINE IS TOO ACID

I have never come across any kit wine that I consider to be too high in acid, nor have I heard anyone else complain on this account. Too high an acid means that too much fruit has been used and manufacturers are unlikely to err in this direction. However, if you feel that your finished wine is too acid add a concentrated solution of two ounces (50 gms) of sugar to the wine after it has been chemically stopped or subjected to pasteurisation. The sugar will simultaneously mask — but not chemically destroy — the acid and create more body, which in turn allows the wine to carry the extra acidity. Alternatively, you may add up to a tablespoon of glycerine (glycerol) per bottle. Although this will slightly sweeten the wine, at this concentration the effect will be minimal and a dry wine will retain much of it sugarless character.

WINE LACKS TANNIN

It is extremely difficult for many people to detect the difference between a lack of acid and tannin. Acid, depending on its type, may be identified as the characteristic sharp taste at the front, middle or back of the mouth. Tannin produces a sensation of dryness around the teeth, gums and inside the cheeks; failure to do this may result in a wine being dull and uninteresting. Tannin can be bought as a solution. Add it dropwise to each bottle, but do take care as it is in a very concentrated form. Once added, excess tannin cannot be removed.

Many unsatisfactory wines lack either tannin or acid and even if you do not necessarily feel that this is the cause of your problem, try adding a little extra of each to a bottle of wine and note the effect. This may be all that you will require to make an ordinary wine into a superb example of the home vintner's art.

WINE LACKS BODY

A wine lacking body will appear to be thin and possess a watery taste. Body is provided by the soluble materials in fruit, unfermented sugar and glycerine. Consequently, adding extra sugar will increase the body in one sense, but unless sufficient other materials are provided by the fruit this will only result in a sweet wine. The maximum quantity of glycerine that you can add is one tablespoon per bottle, otherwise the wine will have a cloying taste. Lack of body results almost entirely from insufficient fruit being used and there is no quick and easy method of overcoming the problem. The answer lies in using the concentrate to make one of the wines given in the recipe section of this book rather than making it up simply as a kit. Where the kit is a compound other than a straight grape juice concentrate it is far more difficult to predict the exact taste that the finished wine will possess. Having experimented with several of the brands which are available, I can confirm that they do give satisfactory results when incorporated with other ingredients.

WINE LACKS BOUQUET AND FLAVOUR

One easy method of giving a bouquet to any white wine is to add half an ounce of dried elderflowers during the fermentation stage. The simplest way of doing this is to make a linen bag about two inches (5 cm) square and fill it with the elderflowers. Suspend the bag from a piece of string into the fermenting bucket or demijohn. The quantity is far smaller than that usually recommended, but the aim here is not to produce an elderflower wine. You will provide the wine with that subtle flower bouquet reminiscent of the Muller Thaugau grape. The subtle flowery aroma is similar in some respects to that of certain German wines.

A can of grapefruit juice will also enhance the flavour of a white wine and, providing it is not drunk for about five months after the fermentation has commenced, you are unlikely to notice the pronounced flavour and bouquet of the added ingredient. Rather, it will give a generally acceptable vinosity.

Lack of flavour in either a white or red wine cannot simply be attributed to the quantity of fruit used in compounding the must. Since all kit wines can support extra fruit you may add a 16 ounce (0.5 kilo) tin of gooseberries to a gallon (5 litres) can of white concentrate. Use both the fruit and the syrup and in your calculations of the total sugar assume that the syrup provides 8 oz (250 gm); any errors involved in this calculation will effect the final alcohol concentration by less than 1% which will be imperceptible.

With red wines you have a wider choice of canned fruits that you may use as additions. Here an 8 oz (250 gm) tin is sufficient as the fruits involved have far stronger flavours. Use either damsons, blackberries or blackcurrants, and assume that the syrup contains 4 ounces (110 gm) of sugar. When using canned fruit in conjunction with concentrates, make the must up in the usual manner in a fermenting bucket and add the fruit and juice. Add the yeast, include pectic enzyme, stir daily and strain the liquid into a demijohn after seven days. Finish the wine by the standard method. For the best possible results it is better to use the concentrate with one of the recipes in this book.

WINE HAS A CHEESE LIKE, VINEGAR OR SIMILAR OFF FLAVOUR

This is due to an infection by a spoilage yeast or bacteria and is the result of poor hygiene. It is sometimes possible to arrest the decay by adding a Campden tablet and potassium sorbate (but do not repeat this procedure if you have already used this technique for stopping the wine). If you do not notice an improvement within a week discard the wine as it will not improve. Next time ensure that all your equipment is completely sterilised.

WINE HAS A MUSTY TASTE

This is due to insufficient racking of the wine. It is not possible to cure this problem in the faulty liquid, so take care with future brews to rack sufficiently early and frequently.

Recipes

NOTE ON UNITS

Currently the United Kingdom is in a transitional state in which items are marketed in metric units or still bear the old Imperial units. In order to minimise the confusion the main units used here are those in which the particular product is marketed. The alternative units are quoted in brackets.

Certain items such as pure grape juice are sold in different sized containers, and where possible I have tried to base the recipes on the size most commonly available. If you do happen to buy a slightly greater quantity then drink or use the extra juice in some other way; do not add the excess to the recipe. Canned fruit is similarly sold in varying amounts. If your can has a weight between 6-10 ounces then use all of the contents where the nominal value of 8 ounces is given in the recipe. Where 16 ounces is quoted any variation between 14 and 20 ounces will suffice.

A can of grape juice concentrate refers to the quantity designed to make one gallon of wine; the actual amount will vary from brand to brand.

The balance of a wine can tolerate relatively large changes in the amount of one ingredient and since most ingredients supply more than one of the components of a wine, the slight variations that do occur should still maintain the high overall quality.

NOTE FOR US WINEMAKERS

The UK gallon is larger than the US gallon, so use the quantities quoted to make either 1.25 US gallons or divide all weights by 0.8 (eight-tenths) to make 1 US gallon.

Rapid Wines

It has long been believed that for a wine to possess real quality it must be stored for a considerable period of time. While this is true of certain styles of wines, others are not only ready for drinking in a far shorter time than the classic reds but they actually begin to deteriorate rapidly. These are those wines that rely on a fruity bouquet and flavour for their attraction. Not only is it possible to drink these wines while they are still young, it is essential if you are to enjoy them at their best. With modern methods it is now possible to make a wine ready to drink within three weeks. There are several different kits available on the market. These are mostly red, white and rosé table wines although it is possible to buy dessert wines that are ready for drinking in a short period of time. *Such kits may be purchased confidently but they should not be adjusted in any way and the instructions should be followed very closely, especially the correct sequence of providing the additives.*

Rapid wines depend for much of their speed of production on the uses of a variety of chemicals; it is possible to buy the chemicals without buying a full kit complete. Kits such as the 'Condessa' can be used with any recipe; here the quality of the wine will depend mainly upon the nature of the ingredients and the formulation that you employ. Packs of this type have the advantage of being cheaper than the full kits and all the benefits of speed; the success of the complete rapid wine kits, however, depends upon the compounding of the juices.

It is also possible to compound your own pack of chemicals effectively, such an approach has a cost advantage and again allows you a complete freedom in your formulation. If you wish to produce your wine in the shortest period of time, however, it is essential that you turn the vast majority of the ingredients in to a liquid before starting the actual process of winemaking.

The only disadvantages to using the rapid approach to winemaking is that wines that are chemically finished to aid clarification frequently possess a chemical, almost peppery, taste — how pronounced this is will depend upon the quantity and type of additives used. Except where special yeasts are used it is difficult to produce alcohol levels much in excess of 12% in under three to four weeks.

Perhaps the real answer for the modern winemaker is to make his wine in about six weeks. This allows most of the advantages of speeded-up fermentations without the restrictions that so often result from a too hasty approach.

SEQUENCE OF OPERATIONS IN RAPID WINEMAKING

When attempting to prepare a wine in the shortest possible time all operations should be directed towards the clarification of the liquid as this is usually the most time-consuming aspect of winemaking.

STAGE 1 Preparing the Liquid

Rapid wine should be made either from juices or a mixture of juices and some solid fruit that has been softened either by boiling or placing in a liquefier. Place the fruit and any solid material in the bucket together with the prescribed amount of water and add one level teaspoonful of bentonite. Bentonite is a white powered clay; the mineral travels up and down the container as a result of the lift brought about by the bubbles of carbon dioxide. As it travels in the liquid its sieve-like structure traps pieces of solid. When carbon dioxide is no longer forming the solid will come to rest at the bottom of the container together with the entrapped vegetable matter. Some winemakers prefer to activate their bentonite the day before it is required, by allowing it to stand in twice its own volume of water. However, this procedure is not essential.

Whether pectic enzyme is used in conventional winemaking will depend entirely upon the nature of the ingredients. Since all fruit contains some pectin which, at the very least, will delay clarification, pectic enzyme should always be added together with the yeast when making rapid wines. There are several yeasts available which ferment very rapidly; these yeasts are the best to use for the quickest possible results. Even if you cannot obtain any yeast other than the standard winemaking variety, however, you can still shorten the working time considerably if you adopt fast ferment techniques.

STAGE II Fast Ferment

The fast ferment technique depends upon a higher temperature than that normally used, commencing the secondary fermentation in the presence of air and regular agitation of the liquid.

When fermenting rapidly, temperatures of 70°-75° F (21°-24° C), as opposed to 65°-70° F (18.5°-21° C) are necessary; this apparently only slight increase in the operating heat has a most profound effect on the speed at which yeast cells build and multiply. A steady temperature should be maintained with all methods of winemaking, but is especially important with this specialised technique. Failure to maintain the temperature will result in the wine being unduly delayed because of a prolonged working period. As the rate of fermentation increases so does the concentration of carbon dioxide and alcohol in the immediate vicinity of the yeast cells. To avoid any danger of a wine's development being retarded as a result of the action of the yeast, the fermentation vessel should be agitated once or twice a day; this will also aid the action of the bentonite.

Prolonged exposure to air will invariably spoil a wine, although with the rapid wine technique this does not present a problem as the liquid will not be remaining under air lock beyond the stage at which carbon dioxide, which protects the wine, is being formed. Throughout the fermentation stage the demijohn should have a one to two inch airspace; the extra air will help to increase the rate of fermentation. When making a wine by the rapid method always add a proprietary yeast nutrient.

STAGE III Stopping the Wine

Another problem avoided by a shorter fermentation period, is that of knowing at which stage to rack. Rapid wines require only one racking — immediately the yeast has finished working. It is important to separate the liquid from the solid as soon as bubbles are no longer seen escaping from the air lock. For at this higher temperature autolysis, the breakdown of dead vegetable material by its own enzymes, will be speeded up to such an extent that spoilage of the wine will be rapid.

Providing that there are no pronounced hazes, the slowest part of the wine clarification process is due to the yeast cells settling out. Wine finings function best if all the yeast cells are dead. To kill the yeast add 1 crushed Campden tablet and 1 gm of potasium sorbate after racking and immediately top up the container with tap water.

Leave the treated wine for 24-48 hours before adding a wine fining agent; those based on chitin (the crushed bodies of shrimp-like animals) are among the most effective. Usually the wine clears within 48 hours; if this fails then immediately repeat the treatment when it will almost certainly clear.

Rapid wines often have a slight chemical taste as a result of the sulphur dioxide added to kill off the final traces of the yeast. If the taste is too strong allow the wine to breathe for two hours before drinking and the artificial flavour will disappear.

DRY WHITE WINE

2 pints (1 litre) apple juice
2 pints (1 litre) orange juice
¾ cup cold tea
1¾ lb (0.75 kilo) white sugar
pectic enzyme
bentonite
Campden tablet/potassium sorbate
wine finings
wine yeast
water to 1 gallon (5 litres)

Dissolve the sugar in a pint of very hot water. Allow to cool, then place in the demijohn together with the cold tea, orange juice and apple juice. Add a teaspoonful of bentonite, the pectic enzyme and the wine yeast. Fit an airlock. Shake the demijohn at least once a day. After a week add water, if necessary, to bring the level up to the shoulder of the container. Return to the warm environment. When bubbles cease, rack. Add the Campden tablet, potassium sorbate and wine finings, then place in the coldest room in the house. Leave for one week. Allow the wine to breathe before serving.

SWEET WHITE WINE

The recipe given below should make 2 gallons of wine.

16 oz (0.5 kilo) can gooseberries
1 can white grape juice concentrate
2 pints (1 litre) pure grapefruit juice
1 cup cold tea
4lb (2.0 kilos)
pectic enzyme
bentonite
2 Campden tablets/2 gm potassium sorbate
wine finings
wine yeast
water to 2 gallons (10 litres)

Separate the gooseberries from the syrup and pour the syrup into a fermenting bucket. Liquidise the gooseberries and transfer the pulp to the bucket. (If you do not have a liquidiser then thoroughly mash the fruit with a fork.) Add the contents of the can of grape juice concentrate together with the washings from the can. Use about 4 pints (2 litres) of water for the washing operations. Also add the grapefruit juice and cold tea. Dissolve 3½ lbs (1.75 kilos) of the sugar in 3 pints of hot water. Allow the syrup to cool slightly, then pour into the bucket stirring vigorously to ensure that localised heat spots, which could lead to the development of pectin, do not occur. Add the bentonite, pectic enzyme and yeast. After leaving for seven days at a temperature of 75° F, strain the liquid and transfer to two demijohns fitted with airlocks. Check that the level of the liquid comes to the shoulder of the vessels. When fermentation ceases rack and stop the wine, but do not top up. Dissolve half a pound (225 gm) of sugar in half a pint (250 ml) of water. Add half of the syrup to each of the demijohns, shake thoroughly and top up with tap water. The extra sweetness will yield a smoother wine which should be ready or drinking about two days later.

ROSÉ WINE

To make 2 gallons of wine

7 oz (200 gm) can blackcurrants
1 can rosé concentrate
2 pints (1 litre) grape juice
2 oz (50 gm) dried elderberries
4 lb (2.0 kilos) sugar
pectic enzyme
bentonite
2 Campden tablets/2 gm potassium sorbate
wine finings
wine yeast
water to 2 gallons (10 litres)

Soak the dried elderberries overnight in a basin, then bring the solid and liquid just to the boil in a saucepan. Simmer for ten minutes or until the berries are soft. Without straining, mash with a fork and add the slurry to the fermenting bucket. Add the syrup from the blackcurrants to the bucket, and liquidise or mash the fruit before adding. Dissolve 3¾ lbs (1.8 kilos) of the sugar in six pints (3 litres) of hot water. Allow to cool slightly before transferring to the fermenting vessel. Add the grape concentrate together with the washings from the can (about 1 pint of water). Add the bentonite, pectic enzyme and yeast. Maintain at 75°-80° F, shaking daily. After four days strain the liquid into two demijohns and after a further four days add tap water until the level of liquid comes to just under the shoulder of the vessel. As soon as carbon dioxide ceases to escape from the airlock, rack and stop the wine with two crushed Campden tablets and 2 gm of potassium sorbate. Two days later add the wine finings together with 2 oz (50 gm) of sugar dissolved in sufficient water to fill each demijohn. Leave for one week before drinking.

DRY RED WINE

8 fl oz (230 ml) blackcurrant juice (Ribena)
8 oz (225 gm) can of blackberries
3½ pints (2 litres) grapefruit juice
½ cup cold tea
1 tbsp glycerine (optional)
2 lb (1 kilo) white sugar
pectic enzyme
bentonite
Campden tablet/potassium sorbate
wine finings
wine yeast
water to 1 gallon (5 litres)

Separate the blackberries from the syrup, mash the blackberries and place together with the syrup and all the other liquid ingredients, into a fermentation bucket. Add the sugar dissolved in one and a half pints of water. Place in a temperature of 75°-80° F and add the pectic enzyme, yeast and bentonite. Agitate daily and strain into a demijohn after seven days. Fit an airlock. Do not top up . After the fermentation ceases treat with a crushed Campden tablet and 1 gm of sorbate. The next day add wine finings, racking into a second demijohn, and add the glycerine. Stop up with a cork or bung and leave for a week, with frequent shaking to ensure that

the glycerine is evenly distributed. Then bottle.

RAPID ELDERBERRY WINE

2 lb (1 kilo) elderberries
2 lb (1 kilo) white sugar
2½ tsps tartaric or citric acid
bentonite
pectic enzyme
wine yeast
Campden tablet/potassium sorbate
wine finings
water to 1 gallon (5 litres)

Elderberries are such excellent winemaking ingredients that no opportunity should be missd to make use of them. The success of the rapid winemaking technique with this particular fruit will depend upon how successfully the liquid can be separated from the skins that contain the slow maturing tannin. The greatest care should be taken with this stage in the preparation. The weight refers to the quantity of fruit after it has been removed from the stalks.

Prepare the fruit by placing in a liquidiser; when all the fruit has been converted into a purée add an equal volume of water and bring just to the boil. Strain the liquid through muslin. Alternatively, crush the fruit with a potato masher and add two pints (1 litre) of boiling water, allow to cool and strain through muslin. When lukewarm place the liquid in the demijohn and add the sugar dissolved in 3 pints (1.5 litres) of water. Check the temperature at 75°-80° F (23°-26° C), add the pectic enzyme, bentonite, wine yeast and citric or tartaric acid.

Top up after five days and finish the wine as described under dry white wine.

BLACKBERRY AND APPLE WINE

3 lb (1.5 kilo) blackberries
2 pints (1 litre) apple juice
2½ lb (1.25 kilo) sugar
2 tsps glycerine
bentonite
pectic enzyme
wine yeast
Campden tablet/potassium sorbate
wine finings
water to 1 gallon (5 litres)

Blackberries, like elderberries, are perfect for making most styles of wine. With blackberries it is the seeds, however, rather than the skins, that must be omitted from the liquid. Crush the blackberries, place them in a container with an equal volume of water and bring just to the boil. Place in a muslin bag and allow to drain overnight. Measure the liquid and add to the apple juice in the fermenting vessel. Subtract the volume of the blackberries' juice from 3½ pints; this is the maximum quantity of water that you can use to dissolve the sugar in. If the volume is less than 1½ pints (0.75 litres), take two pints (1 litre) of the fruit juice, heat on the stove and dissolve in the sugar. Irrespective of how it was prepared add the syrup to the main liquid. At 75°-80° F (23°-26° C) add the bentonite, pectic enzyme and yeast. Finish the wine as described under dry red wine.

CONCENTRATE DRY WHITE WINE

3 cans white grape juice concentrate
16 oz (1 kilo) can gooseberries
2 pints (1 litre) grapefruit juice
2 pints (1 litre) apple juice
3 tsps citric or tartaric acid
4 lb (2 kilos) very ripe bananas
3 cups cold tea
10 lb (5 kilos) sugar
pectic enzyme
amylase
bentonite
Campden tablet/potassium sorbate
wine finings
wine yeast
water to 5 gallons (25 litres)

Select bananas that are overripe, discard the peel and remove any signs of decayed material. Mash the bananas, place in a preserving pan with sufficient water to cover, bring to the boil and simmer gently for twenty minutes. Strain the liquid through muslin, but do not squeeze. Transfer the juice into a fermenting bucket, add the syrup from the gooseberries, the mashed fruit, and the grapefruit and apple juices together with the grape juice concentrate and the washings from the cans. Dissolve the sugar in 10-12 pints (6 litres) of hot water and add to the fruit juices. When cool, add the yeast, pectic enzyme, amylase, acid and cold tea. After one week, strain, make up to 4½ gallons (22.5 litres) with tap water and finish as described under dry white wine.

ECONOMY DRY RED WINE

1 kilo (2 lb) jar bilberries
8 oz (250 gm) dried elderberries
2 cans red grape juice concentrate
3½ pints (2 litres) grapefruit juice
2 pints (1 litre) apple juice
4 tsps citric acid or tartaric acid
10 lb (5 kilos) sugar
bentonite
pectic enzyme
Campden tablet/potassium sorbate
wine finings
wine yeast
water to 5 gallons (25 litres)

Leave the dried elderberries to soak over night
in a pint (½ litre) of water in a basin; then place
solid and liquid in a saucepan and bring to the
boil. Mash the fruit liquid and place the slurry in
the fermenting vessel. Break up the bilberries and
place in the bucket together with the syrup, the
grape juice concentrate, the washings from the
can and the grapefruit and apple juice. Dissolve
the sugar in 12-14 pints (6 litres) of water and
add together with the citric or tartaric acid. Allow
the temperature to reach 75°-80° F (23°-26° C)
before adding the pectic enzyme, bentonite and
wine yeast, making the volume up to 4½ gallons
(22.5 litres). Strain after one week. Finish
according to the method given for dry red wine,
omitting the addition of glycerine.

Dessert Wines

Dessert wines are the fullest of wines; they are high in alcohol and acid although the latter is not a noticeable characteristic. They are also the strongest of all wines. Dessert wines come in two main styles — those resulting entirely from fermentation and those which are fortified by the addition of spirit, usually brandy.

Making this class of wine presents the problem of obtaining sufficient fruit to provide body and the development of a high enough alcohol level. Used on their own the majority of grape juice concentrates cannot provide the wine with everything that it requires. There is only a limited number of commercial dessert wines — and only a small percentage of these could be described as great. The special characteristics of dessert wines require high levels of sugar within the grape. This can be achieved by mould growing on the grapes removing some of the water, water loss through the grape drying on the vine or partial conversion to raisins as a result of sunlight. Occasionally this can result in the wine having a slightly burnt taste. It is this characteristic that the home winemaker can readily imitate by incorporating a small quantity of demerara sugar into his brew.

Glycerine develops naturally in all grapes, and, perhaps more than any other ingredient, is responsible for the depth and body of a wine. To make any style of dessert wine it is necessary to include sufficient glycerine. Large quantities of ripe fruit will usually have adequate natural glycerine; if you are using smaller amounts, however, you may need to add extra glycerine. For the addition of glycerine to be successful it is necessary to restrict the quantity — over treatment will result in a cloying wine. You must also allow the wine to mature long enough for the heavy viscous liquid to dissolve and enter into chemical combination with the other constituents.

FEEDING THE WINE

Providing a quantity of demerara sugar presents no problem. However, if you need to add large amounts of sugar it should not all be added at the commencement of fermentation. Sugar has an affinity for water and if a large concentration is allowed to come into contact with yeast it will draw the water out of the yeast cells and kill the plant. The problem may be overcome by ensuring that at the intitial stage the maximum sugar concentration is not allowed to exceed 3 lb (1.5 kilo) per gallon.

Extra sugar is usually added at the rate of 2-4 oz per gallon only when all the sugar already in the liquid has been converted into alcohol; this process is known as feeding a wine. The need for extra sugar may be checked by tasting the wine or using the hydrometer. Any dessert wine with a gravity below 1.005 may safely be fed without the danger of it becoming oversweet should fermentation not recommence. The tolerance of various strains of yeast varies so it is not possible to say how many feeding operations will be required. The greater the number of feedings the higher the alcohol level — with this particular style of wine this means the better the quality. Where I have indicated a specific number of feedings in a recipe it refers to the number that the yeast can usually tolerate and should only be taken as a guide.

FORTIFYING WINE

Providing that it is sound, free from infections and off flavours any dessert wine will benefit from fortification. However, the expense of spirits tends to deter most winemakers from adding them. Fortunately the quality of the brandy used does not seem to effect the standard of the finished wine; consequently only the cheapest spirit need be used. The highest alcohol level it is usually possible to obtain by fermentation is in the region of 16%. As the majority of fortified wines contain about 18% alcohol only slight additions are required. One fluid ounce of 40% spirit added to 26 fluid ounces (the size of a standard wine bottle) increases the alcohol level by approximately 2%. Calculate the strength of your wine based on hydrometer readings or assume that the wine has a strength of 16%. This will enable you to add the correct amount of brandy.

MATURATION

Dessert wines more than any other style require a long maturation period as time is needed for the high levels of alcohol and acid to marry together. The wines are best stored in bulk in a demijohn. If you wish to speed up the maturation process you can add 'Sinatin 17', an extract of oak barrels; this tends to 'age' the wine and give the typical oak taste that can otherwise only be obtained by genuine barrel maturation.

Since dessert wines require far more fruit than other wines they tend to be the most expensive. While it is possible to make excellent wines very simply, one approach is to use two cans of concentrate instead of one per gallon. This is only really practical with the cheaper low density concentrates, as the higher quality product would contain too much acid and sugar. Every effort has been made to produce reasonably priced recipes; those quoted may appear to be more costly than the majority of homemade wines, but they are still fairly cheap in comparison with a reasonable quality commercial dessert wine.

FULL WHITE DESSERT WINE

To make 2 gallons:

3 cans white grape juice concentrate
3¼ lb (1.6 kilo) white sugar
wine yeast
water to 2 gallons (10 litres)

The quality of the wine will depend very much on the type of concentrate that you use and generally the more expensive the better. When pricing this wine remember that you will be obtaining twelve bottles of top quality wine.

Pour the contents of the cans into a fermentation bucket, together with the washings from the cans. Add 2¾ lb (1.3 kilos) sugar as a syrup dissolved in three pints of hot water. Make up the total volume to 16 pints (10 litres). Check that the temperature is at 65°-70° F and add the yeast. When the initial vigorous yeast head has subsided, transfer to two demijohns and fit an airlock. Maintain at the recommended temperature until fermentation has ceased. The wine is likely to still be dry; if this is so add 2 oz (50 gm) of sugar dissolved in sufficient water to fill the container. Again return to the recommended temperature. Rack again and repeat the feeding until the wine retains sweetness. Store for at least three months before drinking.

RICH GOLDEN DESSERT WINE

1 can white grape juice concentrate
½ lb (250 gm) light coloured sultanas
2 lb (1 kilo) very ripe bananas
1½ lb (0.75 kilo) white sugar
¼ lb (100 gm) demerara sugar
pectic enzyme
amylase
wine yeast
water to 1 gallon (5 litres)

Peel and discard the skins of the bananas, then place with two pints (1 litre) of water in a saucepan, bring to the boil and simmer for 20 minutes. Strain the juice and transfer to the fermentation bucket. Mince or chop the sultanas, add a pint of water and bring just to the boil with constant stirring. Pour the slurry into the fermentation bucket. Add the contents and washings of the grape juice concentrate to the mixture and a pound (0.5 kilo) of white sugar dissolved in a pint of water. Allow the temperature to reach 65°-70° F (18.5°-21° C), then add the yeast, pectic enzyme and amylase. After seven to ten days strain the liquid and transfer to a demijohn and fit an airlock. When the level of sediment reaches a ¼ to ½ an inch thick rack. Dissolve the ¼ lb (100 gm) of demerara sugar in sufficient water to top up, and again return to the warm. Feed the wine as described under Full White Dessert Wine.

RED DESSERT WINE 1

To make 2 gallons of wine

16 oz (0.5 kilo) jar bilberries
1 can grape juice concentrate
½ lb (250 gm) raisins
½ lb (250 gm) sultanas
2 lb (1 kilo) bananas
5 lb (2.5 kilos) sugar
pectic enzyme
wine yeast
water to 2 gallons (10 litres)

Prepare a banana gravy by peeling the bananas, mashing and bring to the boil with two pints (1 litre) of water. Simmer for twenty minutes, strain the liquid into the fermenting vessel and discard the pulp. Mince or chop the sultanas and raisins before placing in the bucket. Dissolve 4 lb (2 kilos) of sugar in 2-3 pints (1-1½ litres) of hot water; transfer the contents of the can and washings into the fermenter, together with the bilberries and their syrup. Make up the total volume to 16 pints (10 litres), check the temperature and add the yeast and pectic enzyme. Strain after seven days and transfer to two separate demijohns fitted with airlocks. Finish by the general method for dessert wines, using the remaining pound of sugar for feeding after racking.

RED DESSERT WINE 2

1 can red grape juice concentrate
⅓ bottle blackcurrant juice (Ribena) or
7 oz (200 gm) can of blackberries
1 lb (0.5 kilo) sugar
1 tbsp glycerine
wine yeast
water to 1 gallon (5 litres)

Dissolve half the sugar in a pint of water. When making the wine with blackcurrant juice, place all the ingredients, except the yeast, blackcurrant juice and glycerine, in the demijohn and make the volume up to seven pints. Check the temperature; when it is between 65°-70° F add the yeast. Top up with water after the initial head has subsided.

If you are using the can of blackberries, you should start the wine in the fermenting bucket. After the initial head has subsided separate the liquid from the solid material and transfer to a demijohn fitted with an airlock. Use the remaining sugar to feed the liquid as necessary. Finally add the glycerine and blackcurrant juice if included.

TAWNY DESSERT WINE

1 can of white grape juice concentrate
1 lb (0.5 kilo) raisins
1 lb (0.5 kilo) can prunes
1½ lb (0.75 kilo) white sugar
½ lb (250 gm) demerara sugar
pectic enzyme
wine yeast
water to 1 gallon (5 litres)

Chop the raisins and bring just to the boil. Transfer the slurry to the fermenting bucket. Add the prunes and the syrup together with the grape juice concentrate and the washings from the can. Dissolve one pound (0.5 kilo) of white sugar and the half pound of demerara in a pint and a half of water; add this to the liquid. When the temperature of the mixture is at 65°-70° F (18.5°-21° C) add the wine yeast and pectic enzyme. After ten days strain, transfer to a demijohn, make up to one gallon with tap water and fit an airlock. Finish as described under Full Red Dessert Wine.

STRAIGHT CONCENTRATE DESSERT WINE

1 can grape juice concentrate
1 lb (0.5 kilo) sugar
1 tbsp glycerine
wine yeast
water to 7 pints (4.5 litres)

Before attempting to make this wine, measure seven pints of water into the demijohn and mark the level on the side of the container with a piece of sticky paper.

Dissolve the sugar in a pint (0.5 litres) of water, and pour the syrup, the concentrate and the washings into the demijohn. Make up to the seven pint mark with water. Add the yeast when the temperature is at 65°-70° F (18.5°-21° C). Allow fermentation to proceed until there is either ¼-½ inch of sediment or until carbon dioxide bubbles can no longer be seen escaping from the airlock. Rack immediately and add ¼ lb (100 gm) sugar dissolved in sufficient water to remake the level to seven pints. When the sugar has been fermented out, detectable again by the cessation of activity, taste. If the wine does not possess residual sweetness then immediately add 2 oz (50 gm) of sugar dissolved in the minimum quantity of water. Continue until the correct degree of sweetness is obtained. Should extra rackings be necessary perform in the usual manner, but only top up to the seven pint mark. After the final racking do not add extra water, but add the glycerine, allow it to marry for a fortnight and then bottle.

This method breaks one of the golden rules of winemaking, never to allow fermentation to take place in the presence of air. It is permissible with a dessert wine, however, because the high concentration of solids will protect it from bacterial attack. Oxygen is unlikely to attack the liquid while carbon dioxide is being formed and even if chemical attack does occur the full-bodied and flavoured desserts can carry it.

Rosé Wines

Rosé wines can be served with fish or meat dishes and they owe much of their popularity to such versatility. Yet there are many people who prefer this middle of the road wine for its own sake. Commercial rosé wines are prepared from red grapes and fermented on the skins for only one or two days, in contrast to the longer period needed in the production of reds. In addition to colouring, some of the flavours characteristic of red wines, although in reduced amounts, go into the make-up of the rosé style. Consequently, it is not sufficient simply to add colouring to a white wine to yield a rosé. It is impossible to imitate the commercial method of fermentation, although with controlled pressings some of the rosé concentrates approximate to the method. The best way for the home winemaker to obtain a rosé wine is to blend together a third of bottle of dry red wine and two thirds of a bottle of white. Providing that the two blending wines have been prepared entirely from grape juice concentrate this method is generally successful. Should either the red or the white wine contain ingredients other than grape, however, they will often react together to give either a haze or a very heavy sediment. This sometimes develops after the wine has been placed in the refrigerator prior to serving.

Rosé wine is so-named from its colour, but the pigmentation is not well defined. Well-known examples of this wine vary in colour from a pale onion skin colour to a deep shade bordering almost on red. Additional colour may be added to the wine with a few drops of cochineal, though this may give an artifical purple tinge.

Rosés are usually drunk medium dry, or in some instances medium sweet. Freshness is part of the character of this wine; to retain this the wine should be drunk after only two months and production should be controlled so that it is never over six months of age before it is drunk. Saccharin is not usually suitable for sweetening wine, because on prolonged storage it gives a bitter taste to the wine, but it may be used with rosés which do not require long maturation periods. Moreover, as only a slight residual sweetness is needed, a half a saccharin tablet per gallon is sufficient and problems are unlikely to develop at this low level of concentration.

One of the most fashionable of drinks is a slightly carbonate rosé; this can be achieved by modifying the technique for producing sparkling wines .

Remember: *under no circumstances should you store rosés in sunlight as they rapidly develop a brownish hue.*

ROSÉ CONCENTRATE WINE

1 can rosé concentrate
8 oz (225 gm) can gooseberries
⅓ cup cold tea
12 oz (330 gm) sugar
½ saccharin tablet (optional)
wine yeast
water to 1 gallon (5 litres)

Transfer the gooseberries and syrup to the fermenting vessel, mashing the fruit with a fork. Add the can of concentrate, the sugar dissolved in a pint of water, the grape juice concentrate and the washings from the can, the cold tea and the half a crushed saccharin tablet — this may be omitted or the quantity doubled according to taste. Check that the temperature is at 65°-70° F (18.5°-21° C) and add the wine yeast. After seven days strain, transfer to a demijohn, make up to one gallon (5 litres) and fit an airlock. Rosé wines made by this method will contain between 10-12% alcohol and should clear immediately after the wine has finished fermenting; this should happen, depending upon the temperature at which the wine has been maintained, after six to eight weeks. If the liquid is not clear at this stage then immediately add wine finings as this type of wine begins to deteriorate rapidly. It is ready to drink as soon as the wine is clear.

ROSÉ WINE FROM WHITE CONCENTRATE

Certain manufacturers of grape juice concentrate do not produce a rosé concentrate, yet sell an excellent white concentrate which you may prefer to use. It may be incorporated in any of the following recipes.

I

1 can white grape juice concentrate
⅓ bottle blackcurrant juice (Ribena)
12 oz (330 gm) sugar
½ cup cold tea
½ saccharin tablet (optional)
wine yeast
water to 1 gallon (5 litres)

Place the grape juice concentrate, the washings from the can, the blackcurrant juice, the cold tea and the sugar as a syrup together with the yeast in a demijohn. Fit an airlock. After the initial fermentation has subsided, top up with water and ferment to dryness. Rack and add the crushed saccharin tablet.

II

1 can white grape juice concentrate
16 oz (0.5 kilo) can damsons
12 oz (330 gm) sugar
½ saccharin tablet (optional)
wine yeast
water to 1 gallon (5 litres)

Pour the damsons and their syrup into the fermentation vessel. Add the grape juice concentrate and the washings, and the sugar dissolved in a pint (0.5 litre) of water. Top up to one gallon if necessary. At 65°-70° F (18.5°-21° C) add the yeast. After five days, or when the initial head has subsided, (whichever is the longer), strain into a demijohn. Fit an airlock. One or two rackings may be required. After the final racking add the crushed saccharin tablet. Leave for one week before drinking.

III

1 can white grape juice concentrate
4 oz (100 gm) dried elderberries or
½ lb (225 gm) fresh elderberries
12 oz (330 gm) sugar
½ saccharin tablet (optional)
wine yeast
water to 1 gallon (5 litres)

Leave dried elderberries to soak overnight in a pint of water. Bring to the boil and simmer for ten minutes. If you are using fresh elderberries, strip them from the stalk, place in the bucket, crush with a potato masher and cover with a pint of boiling water. The following stages are common to both starting ingredients. Add all the ingredients except the yeast and make up to seven pints. At 65°-70° F (18.5°-21° C) add the yeast. After two days, strain and transfer the liquid to a demijohn and fit an airlock. Seven days later top up with water. When the final racking has been performed add the crushed saccharin tablet.

FIVE GALLON ROSÉ SPECIAL WINE

2 cans red grape juice concentrate
3 cans white grape juice concentrate
2 pints (1 litre) orange juice
2 pints (1 litre) grapefruit juice
3 saccharin tablets (optional)
4 lb (2 kilos) sugar
wine yeast
water to 5 gallon (25 litres)

Place the grape juice concentrates and their washings in a five gallon fermentation vessel. Add the orange and grapefruit juice. Dissolve the sugar in four pints of water before adding to the other liquids. Make up the total volume to 40 pints (25 litres) with tap water. When the initial head has subsided transfer to a five gallon fermentation vessel. Rack once or twice as necessary. Add the saccharin tablets and bottle.

Sparkling Rosé

You can use any of the foregoing recipes to make a sparkling wine, or a can of rosé concentrate.

To make a sparkling wine it is necessary to induce a further fermentation, in the bottle, after the wine has cleared and the final racking has taken place. It is essential to use a Champagne bottle or other vessel designed to allow a secondary fermentation, otherwise a breakage may result. It is also advisable to employ a Champagne yeast to ensure that any sediment formed is firm.

Immediately fermentation has ceased check before adding the saccharin that the wine is completely dry; any residual sugar could result in pressure developing which might cause the bottle to burst. It is best to test for dryness with a hydrometer for, unless you have an experienced palate, you may not appreciate exactly what constitutes a completely dry wine. A dry rosé will usually have a gravity below 1.000, often as low as 0.970.

Pour the wine into bottles, leaving an air space of 1½-2 inches (3.5-5 cm). Add a ¼ of a teaspoonful of white sugar — this is half the quantity used for a full sparkling wine as this style of rosé is usually drunk with less effervescence than that produced in a full sparkling wine.

Place the bottles in the same temperature, 65°-70° F (18.5°-21° C), as is used for the main working of the yeast. It is not necessary to add extra yeast; indeed any addition will only add to the sediment at the bottom of the bottle and there will be sufficient cells in the liquid even after it has cleared. There is only a relatively small amount of residual yeast and due to the small ratio of air space to liquid, the plant takes longer than usual to build up to the size of the colony. When the secondary fermentation has finished the yeast has to settle, so although you are adding only a small quantity of sugar allow the wine to stand at the fermenting temperature for 4-6 weeks.

Red Table Wines

Most wine is drunk with meals and most home winemakers will consider a sound stock of red and white table wines in their cellar important. Such large quantities of table wines are consumed that it will pay you to make your wine in five gallon lots either in large carbuoy fermenters or the plastic containers used for selling draught sherry. These may be easily converted into suitable fermentation vessels by removing the centre of the top portion — simply by pushing out — and replacing it with an airlock fitted with a rubber bung. But do not store your wine for prolonged periods in these containers. It is also far cheaper to buy cans of grape juice concentrate designed to make five gallon batches, than single gallon units. Where the recipes are quoted on the basis of five gallon brews, this allows for greater latitude in the choice of ingredients. They can, of course, always be scaled down to make smaller batches.

Characteristics

Before deciding which recipe to use consider which characteristics you require in a homemade red table wine. The majority of vintners will look for a close similarity to the commercial equivalent, but you must bear in mind the limitations of the kitchen method. Unlike the large producers of wine, few people will possess sufficient storage space to allow their wines to mature for even two or three years; they will also wish to enjoy the fruits of their labours in months rather than years. Ideally any homemade wine should be ready for drinking within six months. Few people will wish to go to the expense of barrel maturation, but this can be overcome by the use of an oak extract such as 'Sinatin 7'.

Wine literature abounds with descriptions of wines that have the taste of wild raspberries or vanilla. Whether you prefer these flavours must remain a personal choice, but you may add a quantity of either raspberry or vanilla essence drop wise to individual wines and decide for yourself whether you think such artificial additives are worthwhile. To achieve the best results always make only the smallest of additions; you can always increase the amount in future batches, but it is impossible to remove excess of any flavouring.

The best time to make such additions is immediately prior to bottling. Certain wines are described as having a blackcurrant flavour; this can be achieved by adding half a bottle of Ribena, boiled for fifteen minutes to remove the preservative, to a five gallon wine batch together with the other ingredients at the commencement of fermentation.

Additives can only improve wines which are basically good, and this will depend upon the ingredients used. Since the quality of grape juice concentrates vary so much, unless you know that a particular brand yields a good quality wine, you should only use the concentrate to provide vinosity and body. The main flavour and character will be given to your wine by the other fruits you use. Blackberries fresh or canned, elderberries fresh or dried, bilberries bottled or canned, and damsons all give their own character to a wine and are ideal for making red table wines. You can make economies by replacing at least some of the grape juice concentrate with either apple or grapefruit juice; this will also boost the acidity of the drink.

ELDERBERRY SUPERIOR TABLE WINE

½ lb (250 gm) dried elderberries or 1½ lb (0.75 kilo) fresh elderberries
2 pints (1 litre) grape juice
2 pints (1 litre) grapefruit juice
2 lb (1 kilo) sugar
½ lb (250 gm) sultanas
1½ tsp citric or tartaric acid
wine yeast
water to 1 gallon (5 litres)

If you are using dried elderberries leave them to soak overnight in a pint and a half of water (0.75 litre). Then transfer the berries and the water to a saucepan, bring to the boil and simmer for twenty minutes. Pour the mixture into the fermenting vessel. If you are using fresh berries, strip the fruit from the stalks and put them straight into the fermenting bucket. Add a pint and a half (0.75 litres) of boiling water. Irrespective of the type of elderberries used add the grape juice, the grapefruit juice and the sugar dissolved in a pint (0.5 litres) of water. Mince the sultanas and add to the bulk. At 65°-70° F (18.5°-21° C) add the yeast. Stir daily, strain after five days, transfer to a demijohn and fit an airlock. Ferment to dryness. If the wine proves reluctant to clear, add finings rather than delay clarification.

CONCENTRATE TABLE WINE (Red or White)

5 gallons grape concentrate kit
2 tsps citric or tartaric acid
3 cups cold tea
3¾ lb (1.8 kilos) white sugar
3 tbsps of glycerine (optional)
wine yeast
water to 5 gallon (25 litres)

One of the criticisms often levelled at concentrate wines is that they lack acid and tannin, so tend to be thin. Increasing the astringency may result in a harsh wine. To overcome the problem add glycerine. Make the wine as described on the instructions, but include the extra acid and cold tea. The amount of sugar given in the recipe is also higher than that often quoted in can instructions, But the extra acid, tannin and body will allow the drink to carry this to give a fuller wine. Add the glycerine after the final racking and allow the wine to stand for a week to allow for complete dispersal of the chemical before bottling.

ECONOMICAL RED TABLE WINE

1 can grape juice concentrate
16 oz (0.5 kilo) can blackberries
8 oz (225 gm) can damsons
8 oz (225 gm) can blackcurrants
3½ pints (2 litres) grapefruit juice
6 lb (3 kilos) white sugar
2 tsps citric acid
wine yeast
water to 3 gallons (15 litres)

To make this economical wine, place the fruit and the syrup in a large covered plastic bucket.

Add the grape juice concentrate and the grapefruit juice. Dissolve the sugar into 4-6 pints (2-3 litres) of water, and add this together with the acid to the bucket. Make up to three gallons. At 65°-70° F add the yeast. Strain the fermenting mixture after one week and transfer to three separate demijohns fitted with airlocks. Only one racking should be required. If the wine does not clear add a proprietary fining.

RED CONCENTRATE SPECIAL WINE

2 cans red grape juice concentrate
1 bottle blackcurrant juice (Ribena) or 16 oz (0.5 kilo) can bilberries
½ lb (225 gm) elderberries
5 pints (3 litres) apple juice
10 lb (5 kilos) sugar
7 tsps citric or tartaric acid
pectic enzyme
wine yeast
water to 5 gallons (25 litres)

Allow the elderberries to soak overnight in two pints of water, then bring to the boil and simmer for twenty minutes. Transfer to a five gallon fermenting vessel. Add either the boiled blackcurrant juice or bilberries (but not both), the grape juice concentrate, washings from the cans and the apple juice. Dissolve the sugar in about ten pints (6 litres) of water and then add the tartaric or citric acid. Add sufficient water to make the total volume up to five gallons (26 litres). At 65°-70° F (18.5°-21° C) add the pectic enzyme and wine yeast. Cover the bucket and stir daily. After seven days strain and transfer to a five gallon fermenter. The wine is ready for drinking after the final racking.

BILBERRY TABLE WINE

16 oz (0.5 kilo) jar bilberries
2 pints (1 litre) apple juice
2 lb (1 kilo) very ripe bananas
¼ lb (100 gm) sultanas
2 lb (1 kilo) white sugar
2 tsps citric or tartaric acid
pectic enzyme
wine yeast
2 tbsps glycerine
water to 1 gallon (5 litres)

Peel the bananas and discard the skins; remove any signs of decay, mash the fruit, and place in a saucepan with a pint and a half of water. Bring to the boil and simmer for thirty minutes. Strain, transferring the whitish grey material to the bucket and discarding the fruit pulp. Mince the sultanas and bring just to the boil with half a pint (225 ml) of water. Add the mixture to the banana juice. Next add the apple juice, the bilberries and their syrup together with the sugar dissolved in 2 pints (1 litre) of water. Make the total volume up to 1 gallon (5 litres), then add the pectic enzyme, yeast and acid. After ten days, strain and transfer to a demijohn and fit an airlock. The wine should be clear after its first racking; if it is not, add a proprietary fining.

For a smoother, fuller wine add two tablespoonfuls of glycerine immediately the wine has cleared. Leave for one week and bottle.

SWEET RED TABLE WINES

The secret of slightly sweet red table wines is to ensure that the sweetness is kept at a very low level; indeed the body of a table wine is insufficient to carry a high degree of sweetness anyway. If the wine is going to be drunk soon after it has cleared you may safely add a half a saccharin tablet per gallon prior to bottling. If you wish to store the wine for a longer period it is advisable to add two ounces per gallon of the non-fermentable sugar, lactose. This may be incorporated at any stage from the initial must to bottling. Should you wish, you may sweeten some of your wine at the rate of half a teaspoon of lactose per bottle and leave the remainder dry.

I have seen it suggested on the instructions of some kit wines that a sweet wine can be made simply by incorporating extra sugar in the initial must. This is not a suitable method for a table wine as the extra sugar will ferment out to alcohol. Only after a level of 16% alcohol, far too high for a wine designed to accompany a meal, has been reached will any sweetness remain in the brew.

White Table Wines

White table wines are extremely popular, but they are always the least well made. Failure to produce a satisfactory white table wine has led many would-be winemakers to return to buying all their wine. The failure is usually due to the weakness of the drink which should have an alcohol content of about 10%, often as low as 8% and never more than 12%. Coupled with the low acid level and lack of residual sugar, this wine has far less natural protection than any other and is readily attacked by both bacteria and atmospheric oxidation. Leaving the wine under even the smallest quantity of air, such as in a partially filled demijohn or bottle, can result in chemical spoilage of the liquid in days rather than weeks. Great care should be taken with all wines to ensure hygienic conditions; with white wines failure to follow the correct procedures will result in a liquid destined for the sink.

Because of the susceptibility of white wine to attack, winemakers tend to resort to chemical treatment. While effective when correctly handled these can, however, lead to the development of further off flavours. Chemical treatment disorders are a recent and increasing problem, unknown to the traditional country winemakers. To ensure enjoyable light dry table wine consume the wine soon after clarification.

Grape juice concentrate is the best ingredient to use as the basis of white table wine, but it can be improved with the addition of apple juice, grapefruit juice and particularly gooseberries. Some wines, particularly those prepared from the Muller Thaugau grape variety, have a flowery bouquet. This can be achieved in a homemade wine by adding a small quantity of fresh or dried elderflowers. Remember, the amount used should be far less than for making the country elderflower wine and the petals should not be allowed to remain in the liquid for such a long period.

WHITE DRY TABLE WINE

1 can grape concentrate
1 litre (2 pints) apple juice
1 litre (2 pints) grapefruit juice
4 lb (2 kilos) sugar
2 tsps citric or tartaric acid
1 cup cold tea
4 tbsps glycerine (optional)
wine yeast
water to two gallons (10 litres)

Dissolve the sugar in about three pints (1.5 litres) of warm water, then place in the fermentation vessel. Add the grape juice concentrate, apple and grapefruit juice. Then add the citric or tartaric acid and cold tea, before making the volume up to two gallons (10 litres). Check that the temperature is at 65°-70° F (18.5°-21° C) and add the yeast. After the initial vigorous head has subsided transfer without straining to two separate demijohns and fit airlocks. The wine will need either one or two rackings. After the wine has cleared add the glycerine and top up the demijohns if necessary. Store under airlock for a fortnight, then bottle. The wine may be drunk as soon as it has been bottled.

SUPERIOR WHITE DRY WINE

1 can grape juice concentrate
16 oz (0.5 kilo) can gooseberries
8 oz (225 gm) white sugar
pectic enzyme
wine yeast
water to 1 gallon (5 litres)

Separate the fruit from the syrup, mash the fruit and place it together with the syrup in a fermenter. Dissolve the sugar in a pint of water, add the contents of the grape concentrate can together with the washings. Make up to one gallon (5 litres) with tap water. At 65-70° F (18.5-21° C) provide the pectic enzyme and yeast. Stir daily and leave in the bucket for from seven to ten days. Strain through muslin and transfer to a demijohn. Top up, if necessary, with tap water, fit an airlock and ferment to dryness.

SWEET WHITE TABLE WINE

1 can grape juice concentrate
1½ lbs (0.75 kilos) bananas
2 pints (1 litre) apple juice
12 oz (330 gm) white sugar
2-4 oz (50-100 gm) lactose
pectic enzyme
wine yeast
water to 1 gallon (5 litres)

Use over-ripe bananas. Peel the fruit and discard the skins. Place with a pint and a half of water in a saucepan, bring to the boil and simmer for 30 minutes. Strain the greyish white liquid into a bucket and discard the pulp. Add the apple juice and concentrate together with the washings from the can. Dissolve the sugar in sufficient water to make the total up to one gallon (5 litres). Provide between 2 and 4 ounces of lactose according to the degree of sweetness that you wish to develop in the wine and stir until dissolved. Allow the bucket to stand until the temperature is at 65°-70° F (18.5°-21° C) then add the yeast and pectic enzyme. Allow to ferment in the bucket for one week. Transfer to a demijohn and fit the airlock.

FLOWERY WHITE DRY WINE

1 can grape juice concentrate
1 pint (½ litre) grapefruit juice
¼-½ oz (6-12.5 gm) dried elderflowers
12 oz (330 gm) sugar
wine yeast
wine finings
water to 1 gallon (5 litres)

Prepare a small muslin bag, 2½ inches (7 cm) square and place the elderflowers inside, sealing the top. (The quantity that you use depends on how strongly flavoured you wish the wine to be.) Sew a piece of string about eighteen inches (½ metre) long to one corner of the bag. Transfer the contents of the grape juice concentrate together with the washings to the fermenting bucket. To this add the grapefruit juice and the sugar dissolved in a pint (0.5 litre) of water. Check that the temperature is at 65°-70° F (18.5°-21° C), then add the yeast. Suspend the sachet of elderflowers in the liquid by trapping the piece of string between the bucket and the lid. The slight air gap is unlikely to cause problems as air can only enter during the early stages of fermentation when the wine will be protected by its own carbon dioxide. After three days remove the sachet and discard. If you intend using the bag again ensure that you boil it to sterilise. Allow the liquid to remain in the bucket for a further four days before transferring to a demijohn and fitting an airlock. When dried flowers have been added to a wine, it often fails to clear completely without the addition of wine finings. This should be done according to the manufacturer's instructions when fermentation is complete.

FLOWERY WHITE SWEET WINE

1 can grape juice concentrate
16 oz (0.5 kilo) can gooseberries
2 lb (1 kilo) very ripe bananas
½ oz (12.5 gm) dried elderflowers
12 oz (330 gm) white sugar
2-4 (50-100 gm) lactose
wine yeast
wine finings
water to 1 gallon (5 litres)

Prepare a muslin sachet 3 inches (8-10 cms) square and fill it with the dried elderflowers. Fix a piece of string for suspending the bag. Skin the bananas, remove any signs of decay, mash the sound fruit and bring to the boil with a pint and a half (0.75 litre) of water. Strain the grey liquid into the bucket and discard the pulp. Mash the gooseberries and add together with the syrup to the banana juice. Pour the grape juice concentrate and washings into the bucket together with the white sugar and lactose dissolved in a pint of water. Make the total volume up to one gallon (5 litres), then add the sachet of elderflowers. Allow the mixture to reach the fermentation temperature and provide the yeast and pectic enzyme. After four days remove the elderflowers, then allow the fermentation to continue in the bucket for a further four to eight days, depending upon when the initial fermentation has ceased. Transfer to a demijohn and fit an airlock. Allow fermentation to proceed until bubbles no longer escape from the airlock. If the wine is not clear add wine finings according to instructions as soon as fermentation is complete.

Note On Flowery Wines

The degree of flowery character found in natural grape wines is only slight, yet this should not stop you from developing the degree of flavour that you prefer in your own wines. You may either increase or decrease the quantity of flowers used. This is preferable to prolonging the period that the liquid is exposed to the petals as a long soak results in material dissolving out of the flowers, giving an unacceptable taste and problems with clarification. Shorter soaking of the petals results in inefficient extraction. If you produce a wine that has too strong a flower flavour, blend it with a more bland wine.

GREEN WHITE TABLE WINE

The term green wine does not refer to the colour; it is a wine which is drunk while it is young and still retains some of its unmellowed acid. Some green wines are also drunk while they are petulant — possessing a very slight effervescence. To make a green wine all you need is to add a carton of grapefruit juice to a can of grape juice concentrate. Grapefruit juice will give the wine a pronounced citric acid taste. Pure grape juice provides a flavour more closely related to that of a commercial wine, but does not give the wine as much zest as fruit juice.

1 can grape juice concentrate
1 pint (½ litre) grapefruit juice or
2 pints (1 litre) pure grape juice
1 cup cold tea
16 oz (0.5 kilo) sugar
wine yeast
water to 1 gallon (5 litres)

Place all the liquids in a bucket. Dissolve the sugar in a pint of water and at 65°-70° F (18.5°-21° C) add the yeast. After the initial fermentation has subsided transfer to the demijohn, top up with tap water and fit an airlock. Ferment to dryness.

If you require a slight effervescence in your wine, transfer the liquid to a Champagne or other naturally sparkling wine bottle after clarification. Add to each bottle just the tip of a teaspoon of sugar — you will only require a small quantity of gas to be developed in this style of wine. Cork the bottle and place in a fermentation cabinet or other warm area for a month before serving. NOTE: Do not make this wine unless you like a really dry, fresh wine. Green wines should always be drunk while they are still young.

Some, but not all, white wines are matured in oak barrels for varying periods of time. If you prefer this style of wine then add an oak extract in the recommended quantities to your brew.

Modern Social Wines

Part of the attraction of winemaking has always been the variety of ingredients used: there is a well established country wine list and sooner or later every winemaker will be tempted to make some of the more traditional wines. Of course, by using modern techniques and supportive ingredients it can be slightly more expensive to make country wines than by the older recipes and methods. However, you should be able to balance this against a vast improvement in quality.

While grape juice concentrates appear to be expensive one can may contain the equivalent of three to four times the quantity of grapes present in a pound of sultanas or raisins. Moreover, you will achieve 100% extraction from concentrates while this figure can never be approached when using raisins even after chopping or mincing.

Wines are produced from liquids, and, with a few unavoidable exceptions, it should be the aim of the winemaker to extract all of his fruits to the liquid state. Few people will possess a winepress, the traditional piece of equipment used in winemaking, but they may well have a liquidiser. This will convert the pulp to a liquid, thus aiding the chemical and physical recovery of the extractives during fermentation. Arguably the best method for preparing fruit in the quantity required by the home winemaker is by steam extraction. Correctly used, the effects of heat on the fruit are minimal, while the extraction rate is at a maximum, allowing the use of smaller quantities of fruit. As the skins of the fruit do not come into contact with the freshly formed alcohol, excess quantities of tannin, which delay the maturation process, will not be extracted. One very important advantage of the steam extraction method is that further sterilisation of the fruit is unnecessary.   If you do not possess a liquidiser or steam extractor you can still make country wines by using concentrates, although they may take slightly longer to mature and will be a little less fruity in character. If you are not extracting the fruit first mash or cut it into pieces as small as possible and add sufficient boiling water to cover the solids. Allow for any added water when making the final volume of liquid up to the prescribed amount.Virtually all country wines made from concentrates clear without problem and they may be drunk when six months old or less without the addition of special chemicals.

Under no circumstances should the volume of the wine be allowed to exceed the recommended amount as any excess will be wasted.

APPLE WINE

8-10 apples
1 can white grape juice concentrate
5 lb (2.5 kilos) white sugar
2 tsps citric acid
1 cup cold tea
pectic enzyme
wine yeast
water to two gallons (10 litres)

Extract the liquid with steam, liquidise if you have a sufficiently powerful machine or cut up the fruit and place it in a large bucket. Except where steam is used cover the fruit with boiling water to kill the wild yeasts which would otherwise lead to a cidery taste. While the water is still fairly hot add the sugar and stir to dissolve. Add the grape juice concentrate and the washings from the can, add the tea and acid. Add sufficient water to make the total volume up to 12 pints (7 litres). If steam extraction is used the total volume can be made up to 16 pints at this stage. At 65°-70° F (18.5°-21° C) add the yeast and pectic enzyme, stir and cover. After seven days strain, transfer to a demijohn and top up if necessary. Fit an airlock. Finish in the usual manner.

APRICOT OR PEACH WINE

This same recipe may be used either for peach or apricot wine. Adventurous winemakers may prefer to use a pound each of peaches and apricots.

2 lb (1 kilo) apricots or peaches
4 lb (2 kilos) very ripe bananas
1 can white grape juice concentrate
4¾ lb (2.3 kilos) white sugar
2½ tsps citric or tartaric acid
2 cups cold tea
pectic enzyme
wine yeast
water to 2 gallons (10 litres)

Remove the stones from the fruit before extracting, liquidising or crushing. Add 2 pints (1 litre) boiling water. Peel the bananas, discard the skins, bring to the boil with three pints (1.5 litres) of water and simmer for twenty minutes. Strain the whitish-grey liquid on to the fruit. Add the contents of the grape juice concentrate can and the washings, together with the cold tea and acid. Dissolve the sugar in four pints (2 litres) of water and pour into the bucket. Add a further pint and a half (0.75 litre) of cold water. At 65°-70° F (18.5°-21° C) add the yeast and pectic enzyme. Cover and stir daily. Strain after ten days, transfer equal quantities to two demijohns, top up and fit airlocks. The wine is usually clear after the first racking; if its appearance is not satisfactory after the second racking add a wine fining.

BLACKBERRY WINE

No opportunity should be missed to make blackberry wines, as this fruit is the perfect ingredient which will disguise any imperfections in the grape juice. The range of blackberry wines is almost infinite. The following recipe yields a medium sweet wine which can be drunk at any time of the day.

5 lb (2.5 kilos) fully ripe blackberries
1 can red grape juice concentrate
2 pints (1 litre) apple juice
5 lb (2.5 kilos) sugar
5 oz (135 gm) lactose
pectic enzyme
wine yeast
water to 2 gallons (10 litres)

When using blackberries do not allow the seeds to be in contact with the liquid for too long or the wine will develop a woody taste. Extract the juice by steam or, if you do not possess a steam extractor mash the fruit, cover with boiling water, strain and gently squeeze. Discard the solid. Whichever method you use measure the volume of liquid that you obtain and use this in your calculation of the total amount of water to add in the later stages.

Pour the blackberry liquid into the fermentation vessel together with the apple juice, the grape juice concentrate and the sugar, including the lactose, dissolved in three pints (1.5 litres) of water. Add sufficient tap water to make the total volume up to two gallons (10 litres). At 65°-70° F (18.5°-21° C) add the yeast and pectic enzyme. After the initial vigorous head has subsided, transfer to two demijohns and fit airlocks.
Note: If you do not use lactose the wine may be sweetened by the addition of a small quantity of sugar solution prior to serving. Do not use saccharin for sweetening as it may result in the development of a bitter taste.

This wine will improve and keep for two to three years.

ELDERBERRY WINE

3½ lb (1.75 kilo) elderberries
1 can red grape juice concentrate
2 pints (1 litre) grapefruit juice
4-6 oz (100-150 gm) lactose (optional)
2 tsps citric or tartaric acid
5 lb (2.5 kilos) white sugar
2 tbsps glycerine (optional)
pectic enzyme
wine yeast
water to 2 gallons (10 litres)

Steam extract the berries or mash the fruit and cover with a quart (2 litres) of boiling water. Leave until cool enough to handle, then strain into a fermenting bucket. Do not liquidise the fruit as the tannin rich skins will remain with the juice and produce a harsh wine. Add the grapefruit juice and the acid. Dissolve the sugar in five pints (3 litres) of warm water before adding to the other liquids. The finished wine will be medium-bodied and can be drunk either sweet, medium or dry. If you prefer a medium wine add 4 oz (100 gm) of lactose; for a sweet wine add 6 oz (150 gm) to the mixture. Add the grape juice concentrate and make up the total volume to two gallons. Add the yeast and pectic enzyme. Maintain at 65°-70° F (18.5°-21° C); when the vigorous fermentation has subsided transfer to two demijohns fitted with airlocks. After the final racking glycerine may be added to give a fuller smoother wine.

GOOSEBERRY WINE

1½ lb (0.75 kilo) gooseberries
1 can white grape juice concentrate
½ cup cold tea
1½ lb (0.75 kilo) white sugar
pectic enzyme
wine yeast
water to 1 gallon (5 litres)

Top and tail the gooseberries, place in a saucepan, cover with water and bring to the boil. Transfer to a fermenting bucket. Add the cold tea and the sugar dissolved in two pints of water. Add the grape juice concentrate and washings, taking care that the total volume does not exceed seven pints (4.5 litres). At 65°-70° F (18.5°-21° C) add the wine yeast and pectic enzyme. Stir daily to mash the fruit. After seven days transfer to a demijohn, top up and fit an airlock. This particular wine may be fed until it is a full dessert.

PLUM OR GREENGAGE WINE

3 lb (1.5 kilo) plums or greengages
1 can white grape juice concentrate
12 oz (330 gm) sugar
2 lb (1 kilo) bananas
pectic enzyme
wine yeast
water to 1 gallon (5 litres)

Either place the plums in a steam extractor, or remove the stones from the plums and bring just to the boil with a pint (0.5 litres) of water. If it is impossible to remove the stones completely, bring to the boil and transfer the liquid, fruit, and stones to a bucket. Continue with the rest of the procedure, but strain to remove the stones as soon as they separate from the fruit tissue, usually after three to four days. Prepare the bananas by skinning and leaving in the refrigerator for 48 hours prior to being required.

Place the plums, their juice, the bananas and any juice, the grape juice concentrate and dissolved sugar in water. Check the temperature and add the yeast and pectic enzyme. Strain into a demijohn after seven days. The wine may be fed with sugar to increase the sweetness and body if necessary.

RASPBERRY WINE

2 lb (1 kilo) very ripe raspberries
1 can of rosé, white or red grape juice
concentrate
12 oz (330 gm) sugar
pectic enzyme
wine yeast
water to 1 gallon (5 litres)

Raspberries with their acid and characteristic flavour are the ideal additive for any grape juice concentrate. When used with a white they produce a rosé, incorporated with a rosé the colour becomes more pronounced and with a red the finished wine has a most definite subtle raspberry character.

Steam extract, liquidise or simply mash the fruit, and add to the concentrate. Add sugar as syrup and make up the total volume to one gallon before adding the yeast and pectic enzyme. If you have not used steam extraction the fruit should be covered with a pint of boiling water and the whole should be strained after three days to remove the seeds which would give the wine a woody taste. When the initial fermentation has subsided transfer to a demijohn and ferment to dryness. Do not attempt to feed this wine as it has insufficient body to provide the ingredients to carry extra sugar as alcohol.

SLOE WINE

2 lb (1 kilo) sloes
1 can red grape juice concentrate
12 oz (330 gm) sugar
2 tbsps glycerine (optional)
2-4 oz (50-100 gm) lactose (optional)
pectic enzyme
wine yeast
water to 1 gallon (5 litres)

Sloes make one of the most popular of country wines, but unless used correctly the resultant drink may be extremely harsh. Do not gather the sloes until they are fully ripe and have begun to wither. Bring the fruit just to the boil with a pint of water, transfer to the bucket and add the grape juice concentrate and sugar as syrup. If you are serving the wine as a medium sweet it may be drunk earlier than the dry wine which often retains its astringency for several months. To sweeten add 2-4 oz (50-100 gm) of lactose with the other ingredients. Check that the volume makes one gallon (5 litres) and that the temperature is at 65°-70° F (18.5°-21° C). Then add the yeast and pectic enzyme. After 3-4 days the stones will have separated from the solid fruit. Strain into another bucket or straight into the demijohn after the initial head has subsided. Ferment until bubbles are no longer seen leaving the airlock. Taste the wine. If it is still harsh and you wish to drink the wine immediately add two tablespoons of glycerine.

Sparkling Wines

Home winemakers are reluctant to make sparkling wines, believing them to be difficult. It is true that you need to pay far more attention to technique, to the selection of the yeast and need the correct bottles, yet if you are prepared to take the care necessary to make any wine correctly you will experience no difficulty in preparing your own sparkling wine. If these wines require more effort than others, then the rewards are certainly greater — no celebration is complete without a bottle or two of 'Bubbly'.

To progress from still to sparkling wines, it is necessary to be able to produce the correct degree of effervescence in the bottle, without transferring a large quantity of yeast sediment which will result in a cloudy wine. This can only be achieved if a carefully controlled secondary fermentation is induced to occur in the bottle. This means that you must know the exact amount of fermentable sugar present — too much could result in a burst bottle, while too little will fail to provide enough carbon dioxide. You will also need to use a yeast which yields a firm sediment.

Ideally you should plan to make a sparkling wine at the outset rather than select one which you feel will improve with the addition of gas. Sparkling wine definitely benefits from the use of a regional yeast; a Champagne yeast will form a firmer sediment than some of the general wine yeasts so ensure that this type is added to the original must. Make sure that you add pectic enzyme as rapid clearing is important. If the wine has not completely cleared to give as brilliant a finish as a commercial wine within a fortnight of gas ceasing to escape from the airlock, then add a proprietary wine fining.

If any sugar remains after fermentation in the demijohn has ceased, it will be converted to gas in the bottle and possibly burst it. To avoid this danger it is necessary to measure the gravity with a hydrometer. Do not rely on taste for, unless you are very experienced, you will not be able to differentiate between a completely dry and a medium dry wine; the latter may in fact contain appreciable amounts of sugar. The gravity of a completely dry wine is usually about 0.996, but may be as high as 0.998. The reason that the figures are below 1.000 is that alcohol itself has a gravity of 0.88 and as the sugar content decreases the alcohol rises; the density you are measuring is of a mixture of alcohol and water. The variation in gravity in different wines is due to the gravity of non-fermentable material present.

Use only genuine champagne bottles for

making sparkling wines; these weigh about 900 gms and many can withstand pressure of up to seven atmospheres. There are other types of bottles for sparkling wines on the market and while some are designed for in-bottle fermentation, a large number are used for artificial carbonation, in which carbon dioxide is injected under pressure into the wine. Using this method it is possible to exert a critical control on the amount of gas that enters the vessel and a lighter weight bottle, often below 400 gms, is used. Even taking all precautions one cannot guarantee that the gas generated by in-bottle fermentation will not exceed the amount that these weaker bottles can withstand. Before using any bottle check carefully for cracks or chips; such points of weakness can lead to explosions.

Wine from a gallon demijohn will fill five bottles, so select and sterilise that number. Prepare a sugar syrup solution by dissolving five 5 ml teaspoonfuls of white sugar in the minimum quantity of water (12.5 ml) and add exactly a fifth (7.5 ml or 1½ teaspoonfuls) into each bottle. Fill the bottle with wine to within an inch of the top (2.5 cm). It is necessary to wire the corks down to stop them blowing as a result of the pressure generated. This is achieved by fixing a collar of packing case type wire around the neck of the bottle. A second piece of wire is hooked under the opposite side of the collar and tightened. The process is repeated with a second piece of wire so that a cross is formed at the top of the cork.

Where artificial clarification by the addition of finings is adopted, often insufficient yeast cells will remain to restart the fermentation and this is one of the few occasions when it is useful to employ a starter bottle. Sterilise a one pint bottle and place 2 oz (50 gm) of sugar dissolved in half a pint of water in the bottle. Add a quarter of a level teaspoonful of citric acid and the tip of a teaspoonful of yeast nutrient. Then add a sachet of Champagne yeast, cover with cling film and leave at the fermentation temperature 65–°75° F (18.5°–21° C) until a vigorous effervescence is noted. At the height of the effervescence add one fluid oz (20–330 ml) of the starter mixture to each bottle. The stage at which the starter is ready will dictate when the bottling operation may begin. In order to avoid an unnecessary waste of time, and the danger of unprotected wine, plan your operation so that the yeast starter, which usually requires 24–48 hours to effervesce, is ready when required. Do not be tempted to add the dry yeast straight into the bottles as it requires far more oxygen to commence breeding then it is likely to find in the bottle wine.

You may find that you have a large quantity of liquid remaining in the starter bottle, on the basis of "waste not want not" use this to start another batch of wine. Champagne yeast can be used to ferment any must and the resultant wine will taste the same as that prepared with conventional general purpose yeast. When you have prepared a must simply tip the contents of the bottle into the bucket instead of adding the solid dried yeast.

Once the cork has been sealed into position, return the bottles to the fermentation temperature which should ideally be between 60°–65° F (16.0°–18.5° C). The lower the temperature the greater the quantity of gas that will dissolve in the wine, a process which will be helped by a slower fermentation rate. Do not be tempted to drop below 60° F (16.0° C) as the yeast may cease working. Under no circumstances should the fermentation temperature rise above 70° F (21° C). Allow the wine to remain at fermentation temperature for at least two months and ideally three. At the lower temperature fermentation will be slower and the conditions in the liquid, with its increasing alcohol strength and the rising gas pressure, are far from ideal for the yeast.

SERVING

There are two ways of dealing with the wine. The simplest and probably the most popular method is to place the bottle in the refrigerator about four hours before it is required. Under no circumstances attempt to serve this style of wine without refrigerating, the higher the temperature the less soluble the gas and warm wines will froth out of the bottle, losing almost all of their gas immediately. You may store the bottles in the refrigerator, providing you do not keep them in a deep freeze. Wines poured straight off the sediment in this way may be kept for about three months after the in-bottle fermentation is complete. Beyond this date the yeast at the bottom of the container will begin to decompose and give the wine a musty flavour. When serving a wine which has a yeast sediment be careful not to shake the bottle and take care with the pouring to avoid disturbing the sediment. You should be able to serve virtually all of the wine, with only the minimum of cloudiness due to yeast disturbance.

DEGORGING

There is a way, based on the champagne method, of removing the yeast and re-sealing the wine so

that it can be stored for several months or even years. However, it may take two or three bottles until you master the knack, so be prepared for wastage. Be sure to perform the operation over a sink!

During the final stages of the maturation process, store the botttles upside down, so that the sediment lies in the neck of the bottle. When the bottle fermentation is complete transfer the bottle (again upside down), with the minimum amount of disturbance, to the refrigerator. Next day take the bottle, keeping it upside down and turn it on its side over the sink. Carefully remove the cork holding the wine and allow the pressure of the gas to force out the sludge. Immediately recap and wire the cork down again. It is of course important that a minimum of liquid is lost during the operation.

The whole procedure is made much simpler if you use 'Vintraps', marketed by Southern Vineyards; these consist of a plastic combined sediment trap and stopper together with the necessary wiring for the bottle. Used with their sparkling wine concentrates or with any other compounded recipe they represent an easy method of making a sparkling wine. As with all proprietary equipment they should be used according to the instructions provided.

EFFERVESCENCE

Part of the beauty of true Champagne is the length of time that the head of bubbles continues to escape from the liquid. This is due in part to the complex chemistry of carbon dioxide and its ability to be retained by certain components present in the wine. Homemade sparkling wines seldom retain their sparkle in the glass for such a prolonged period, but they will continue to effervesce for many minutes. The problem of prolonged retention of gas has not been completely solved for home winemakers — the answer appears to be partly in the ingredients used and partly in the maturation period, which is probably far longer than most of us would wish to wait. Very few winemakers will be dissatisfied with the standard of effervescence. If you prefer more bubbles, however, do not increase the sugar content under any circumstances; this will only result in a greater degree of froth and in most cases broken bottles!

ARTIFICIAL CARBONATION

The recent appearance of machines for making soft drinks has led to a method of carbonating wines artificially. Select the wine that you wish to carbonate and allow it to stand in the refrigerator for twenty four hours. Then fill the water compartment of the drinks maker with the wine. Fill the machine with carbon dioxide according to instructions and serve the drink from the dispenser into a wine glass. Drinks prepared in this manner have quite a sparkle. The method has the advantage that any bottle of wine may be used and that no special preparations are necessary.

SWEETENING SPARKLING WINES

In order to avoid complications when you are determining the gravity of the wine, the sweetening agent should be placed in the bottle before pouring the wine in. As the in-bottle period can be fairly long and the wines are extremely delicate, revealing any off flavours, you should avoid using saccharin. Sweeten the wine by dissolving one level teaspoonful of lactose in the minimum amount of water and add together with the priming sugar solution. This quantity of sugar may be halved or doubled in subsequent brews.

Due to their method of production and because the wines are stored under carbon dioxide, attack by bacteria and spoilage yeast are far less likely to occur than with tables wines. This does not mean, however, that you can take less care with hygiene, but you can make wines of a lower alcohol content.

SPARKLING WINE 1

1 can grape juice concentrate
2 pints (1 litre) apple juice
8 oz (225 gm) white sugar
pectic enzyme
champagne wine yeast
water to 1 gallon (5 litres)

Dissolve the sugar in half a pint of water, and place it with the apple juice and grape concentrate in the demijohn. Make up the volume to three quarters full with tap water. At 65°-70° F (18.5°-21° C) add both yeast and pectic enzyme. Top up with tap water when the initial fermentation has subsided. When gas can no longer be seen escaping from the airlock check the gravity; if it is below 1.000 add a proprietary finings. When clear transfer to champagne bottles and induce fermentation in the bottle by the method described above. The wine may be sweetened by the addition of lactose if required.

SPARKLING WINE 2

2 pints (1 litre) pure grape juice
16 oz (0.5 kilo) can gooseberries
1½ lb (0.75 kilo) white sugar
5 tsps lactose (optional)
pectic enzyme
champagne yeast
water to 1 gallon (5 litres)

Place the gooseberries and their syrup in a sterilised bucket. Mash the fruit with a fork or a potato masher. Add the grape juice and the sugar dissolved in 2 pints of warm water. Add a further 3 pints of cold tap water and thoroughly stir the mixture. Allow the mixture to come to 65°-70° F (18.5°-21° C) before adding the pectic enzyme and wine yeast. After seven days strain the liquid through muslin and transfer to a demijohn, top up with tap water and fit an airlock. Check the gravity when carbon dioxide can no longer be seen escaping from the airlock. Only if gravity is below 1.000 can you proceed to clarify the wine if necessary, and bottle according to the general instructions for the type of wine.
Note: Very occasionally any wine will prematurely cease fermentation. Should this happen to this particular wine, then drink as a sweet white table rather than proceeding to produce a sparkle.

SPARKLING RED WINE

This is not a generally recognised wine, but you may if you wish treat any of the dry red table wines by the method described above. Alternatively, they may be served from a fizzy drinks machine.

SPARKLING ROSE — *See under Rosé Wine*

Aperitifs

An aperitif is a wine designed to be drunk before a meal. While the individual may drink any wine he chooses to stimulate his appetite two general styles of aperitifs are recognised: the oxidised wines of the sherry style and the herb wines of the vermouth style. Both these wines trigger off the digestive juices with their high alcohol level, and dry oxidised or bitter taste. Sweet tastes tend to suppress the digestive system and this is one of the reasons why heavy dessert wines are consumed at the end of the meal.

VERMOUTH

This style of wine owes its character to the blend of herbs, the most pronounced of which is wormwood, which gives the wine its bitter taste, coupled with high levels of alcohol and acid. Fortification, which in this case would be wine-based spirit, cannot be justified on the grounds of cost. Since many of the commercial herb-type wines contain in the region of 18% alcohol, only 2% above the 16% fermentation value, it is possible to make a vermouth style wine without recourse to expensive spirit.

In addition to compounding the must correctly a further complication exists with vermouth preparation — that of obtaining the correct blend of herbs. The composition of the herbs used in the commercial drinks of this style is a closely guarded secret; the major firms successfully keep their precious formulae away from the eyes of their competitors. Homebrew suppliers have now developed a range of different blends and the best advice is to test a variety of these.

There are two methods of making this style of wine. The first recipe uses a vermouth concentrate and the second either a red, white or rosé wine base with the addition of a vermouth flavouring.

When using a concentrate, you may wish to increase both the acid and alcohol level; the answer is to incorporate a litre of grapefruit juice. The citric acid, rather than detracting from the flavour of the wine, actually appears to increase the bitterness and sharpens the drink. Alcohol level can be built up very easily, by simply adding 2 oz of sugar dissolved as a syrup as soon as fermentation ceases. Check with the hydrometer, however, that the gravity has dropped below 1.000 before you make any addition; failure to do this can result in the wine not refermenting. Obviously there is a stage at which no more sugar will ferment and the wine will have a very slight residual sweetness. Vermouths are in fact seldom drunk absolutely dry, and at the concentrations at which the sugar is being fed you should achieve the medium dry effect that is necessary to balance the other strong flavours. Inevitably some winemakers will not be fully satisfied with the flavour of their vermouth. Flavour can only be adjusted by the provision of extra herbs. These can either be added to a proprietary vermouth concentrate or any other wine base.

Drinking fashions change and today the commercial vermouth producers market whites, red and rosés, both sweet and dry. Most commercial vermouths are prepared by the infusion of herbs into a wine and this technique can be readily adopted. Add the herbs to the wine after fermentation is complete by preparing an infusion bag about 2 inches (7 cm) square from tight woven nylon material. Attach to it a piece of string about one foot (30 cm) in length, place a vermouth flavouring powder, sufficient for one gallon of wine, in the bag and sew up. Insert the bag in the wine and trap the string with the fitted cork. Leave the wine at room temperature for a month, take a sample and taste. If the wine has sufficient herb flavouring, then remove the bag and bottle the wine; if the flavour lacks depth keep the bag in the wine for a further month. Top up the wine with tap water after sampling. If the wine still lacks flavour after two months it is unlikely to acquire the correct flavour simply by allowing the herb to remain in contact with it. Try either a different blend of herbs (in a new sample of base wine) or use a larger amount of the powder with your next brew.

To prepare a vermouth it is necessary to make a base wine of high alcohol content; the same base wine may be used for a dry or medium dry vermouth.

WHITE BASE WINE (Sweet or Dry)

2 pints (1 litre) can grape juice concentrate
2 tsps citric acid
sugar to a maximum of 2 lb (1.6 kilo) (see below)
vermouth style flavouring powder (herbs)
pectic enzyme
wine yeast
water to 1 gallon

Dissolve one pound of the sugar in a pint of hot water, allow to cool and place in the demijohn together with with grape juice concentrate and citric acid. Add the pectic enzyme and yeast, adjust the level if necessary to just above the shoulder of the demijohn and fit an airlock when the initial fermentation has subsided. Top up with tap water.

When gas bubbles are no longer seen to escape from the airlock, rack and, if making a dry wine, add a further 2 oz sugar dissolved in the top up water; for a sweet wine base add twice this quantity of sugar. After checking with the hydrometer make additions of the same quantities of sugar syrup each time fermentation ceases. Providing that only a small quantity of sediment has formed it will not be necessary to rack each time additions are made; simply remove sufficient liquid to allow room for the syrup. At the completion of fermentation the sweet wine will contain a residual amount of sugar of 4 oz (100 gm) or less; the wine may be sweetened further to taste. The medium dry base will contain not more than 2 oz (50 gm) per gallon. Infuse the herb powder as described above.

ECONOMY WHITE BASE WINE (Sweet or Dry)

2 pints (1 litre) can white grape juice concentrate
2 pints (1 litre) grapefruit juice
sugar to a maximum of 2½ lb (1.25 kilo)
vermouth style flavour powder (herbs)
pectic enzyme
wine yeast
water to 1 gallon (5 litres)

Make the wine as described above but increase the amount of sugar initially added from 1 lb to 1½ lb (0.5 to 0.75 kilo).

ECONOMY RED BASE WINE (Sweet or Dry)

2 pints (1 litre) can red grape juice concentrate
1 tsp citric acid
½ cup cold tea
sugar to a maximum of 2 lb (1 kilo)
vermouth style flavour powder (herbs)
pectic enzyme
wine yeast
water to 1 gallon (5 litres)

Make the wine as described under White Base Wine (sweet or dry), adding the cold tea together with the grape juice concentrate.

ECONOMY ROSÉ BASE WINE (Sweet or Dry)

1 litre (2 pints) can white grape juice concentrate
16 oz (0.5 kilo) can raspberries
1 tsp citric acid
½ cup cold tea
sugar to a maximum of 1¾ lb (0.75 kilo)
vermouth style flavour powder
wine yeast
water to one gallon (5 litres)

Mash the raspberries in a bucket, add the syrup and the grape juice concentrate and ¾ lb (330 gm) of the sugar dissolved in a pint (0.5 litres) of water plus three pints of cold water. At 65°-70° F (18.5°-21° C) add the yeast, pectic enzyme, cold tea and citric acid. After seven days strain, transfer to a demijohn, top up with tap water, if necessary, and fit an airlock. When fermentation ceases, rack and top up with 2 oz (50 gm) of sugar dissolved in water if making a dry wine, or 4 oz (100 gm) of sugar for a sweet wine. Repeat the process each time fermentation ceases until the yeast has finished working. Add the vermouth powder as described earlier.

Vermouth type Concentrates

There are a number of vermouth type concentrates available, these can be adjusted to improve the quality by using the general techniques described for commercial concentrates.

Sherry

To understand the problems of home sherry production it is necessary to know how the commercial wine is made. Although there are operations such as to 'soleraing' the wines, where young wines are stored with old to ensure the continuation of style over the years, at the heart of sherry production is the stage during which fermentation is completed at least partially in the presence of air. During this stage fungal growth, or flor, can occur on the top of the wine; this is responsible for the uniqueness of the taste and aroma of sherry for certain compounds in the wine are oxidised during flor growth. It is perhaps not true to say that the flor will not grow in this country, but it will certainly not develop simply by leaving the bung out of the demijohn. All that would result from such an approach would be the the growth of 'flowers of wine', which destroys the alcohol present, or a vinegar-forming yeast. A sherry-style wine can be made in the home without the flor, providing air is allowed to come into contact with the liquid. However, air should only be allowed to come into contact with the liquid when bacterial and yeast growths are impossible, that is when the alcohol level has reached 15-16%. Sherry is another example of a fortified wine and this level

of spirit is needed.

Oxidation is best achieved by removing the equivalent of a bottle of liquid after fermentation has finally ceased and fitting the top of the demijohn with cotton wool. It is debatable whether the wine should be racked before or after oxidising — in the commercial operation the young sherry is still standing on part of its lees while the oxygen is intereacting. My personal view is that at home it makes very little difference whether you rack before or after oxidation is complete as you will have already performed at least one racking before fermentation will have ceased.

In all forms of winemaking whether it involves thousands of bottles on a commercial scale or just one or two at home the quality of the final wine will depend upon the acquired skill of the vintner; nowhere is this more important than with home sherry production. While the sherry is standing in the demijohn under air you must take out a sample and taste it every week. As soon as you are convinced that you have the correct degree of sherry-type flavour stop the process by refilling the demijohn with the sample of wine that you originally removed from the liquid. Make up the quantity lost through sampling the liquid by adding tap water. As with many wines part of the flavour is due to the oak barrel taste, so to ensure a close imitation add some oak extract.

With all wines which are fed to increase the alcohol level it is not always possible to guarantee that a wine will finish absolutely dry. This again has a parallel in the commercial field where vintners can never be absolutely sure what style of wine will result from each fermentation; the great sherries are a result of highly skilled blendings. If you want to ensure that the wine is dry then after you have added 1¾ lb (0.8 kilo) only add the rest of the sugar in 2 oz (50 gm) portions. Occasionally fermentation will restart if the wine is left for about a week under air in a warm temperature; the extra oxygen allows the yeast to go to its absolute limit in spirit production and all wines become slightly drier on standing. If fermentation restarts and you require a sweet wine do not add extra sugar until the oxidation process is over and the liquid has been recombined, otherwise a slow fermentation, which yields carbon dioxide and arrests oxidation, may continue for months. Sweet sherries are noted for their smoothness and this cannot be achieved by the addition of 4 oz (100 gm) of sugar to the gallon alone. While still in the demijohn add four tablespoons of glycerine and allow to stand at least a month with constant shaking so that the liquids mix thoroughly. Sherry benefits from a long bulk storage before bottling.

Kits are available containing flavourings. They will not need the oxidation treatment; indeed it may even be harmful if the alcohol level developed is not adequate high to give sufficient protection. So if you are using a blended sherry kit follow the instructions. To prepare a sherry from a grape juice concentrate use the following procedure.

SHERRY

1 can white grape juice concentrate
1½ tsp citric or tartaric acid
½ cup cold tea
2 lb (1 kilo) sugar
glycerine (optional for sweet sherry)
wine yeast
water to 1 gallon (5 litres)

Place the grape juice concentrate, 1¾ lb (0.8 kilo) of the sugar dissolved in two pints of water and the cold tea in a bucket. Make up to 7½ pints (4 litres) and add the yeast. After ten days transfer to a demijohn, add a further quarter of a pound of sugar dissolved in sufficient water to top up the container and fit an airlock. Ferment to dryness and rack. If making a sweet sherry add a further quarter of a pound of sugar as syrup or, for a dry sherry, a further 2 oz (50 gm) and again ferment. If the wine remains dry after fermentation ceases repeat the last step until such time as there is either a pronounced sweetness, or only a slight trace of sweetness for a **medium** sherry. Remove the airlock and a bottle of the wine; fill with a cotton wool plug. After a fortnight sample a very small quantity of the wine. Repeat this procedure at fortnightly intervals until the correct degree of oxidation is obtained. Then recombine the wine in the bottle with that in the demijohn. Rack if necessary. If making a sweet wine add the glycerine. Store in bulk before bottling.

Original Wines

Winemaking is nothing if not fun, and you will miss some of the pleasure if you do not wander down the wine byways. Although the idea of making a wine from every non-poisonous plant known is old-fashioned and the resultant drinks are strange, to say the least, there are some ingredients which at first sight possess no winemaking potential but which nevertheless yield a most interesting wine. It is often impossible to categorise these wines into table, dessert or social; they are simply to be enjoyed. Experimenting with new wines can result in disappointments which cannot always be rectified by blending, so unless you wish to make winemaking a major pastime and you have a large enough cellar to cater for the forseeable future I would advise you to restrict your original wines to those given below. You can of course improve them by adding extra acid, sweetening or blending or using any other corrections suggested for wines in general.

GUAVA WINE

16 oz (0.5 kilo) can guavas
2 pints (1 litre) apple juice
24 fl oz (0.7 litres) white grape juice
1 lb (0.5 kilo) white sugar
½ cup cold tea
pectic enzyme
wine yeast
water to 1 gallon (5 litres)

Separate the guavas from the syrup and mash the fruit with a fork — the seeds will not have an adverse effect on the wine. Add the grape juice and the apple juice and a half pound of sugar dissolved in a pint of water. At 65°-75° F (18.5°-21° C) add the yeast, pectic enzyme and cold tea. Allow to ferment for four days, strain into a demijohn and fit an airlock. Five days later, when the vigorous ferment has subsided (if it has not, delay until there is just a controlled escape of carbon dioxide), strain and transfer to another demijohn. Dissolve the remaining sugar in sufficient water to top up the demijohn. Fit an airlock. Ferment to dryness. This wine has a delicate taste and bouquet which is destroyed if the wine is oversweetened; any addition of sugar to taste should be kept to a minimum. Drink the wine while still young.

PRUNE AND DATE WINE

1 lb (0.5 kilo) prunes
1 lb (0.5 kilo) dates
2½ lb (1.25 kilo) white sugar
2½ tsps citric acid
pectic enzyme
amylase
wine yeast
water to 1 gallon (5 litres)

Use slabs of dates. Break up the dates and place in a basin with a pint of water; place the prunes in a basin and treat similarly. Combine the two mixtures in a saucepan and bring just to the boil, stirring to ensure that none of the fruit sticks to the pan. Remove the pan from the heat as soon as the liquid boils. Allow to cool and transfer to the bucket, dissolve the sugar in a pint and a half (0.75 litre) of hot water, make up the total volume to one gallon, add the acid and check the temperature. At 65°-70° F (18.5°-21° C) add the yeast, pectic enzyme and amylase. Stir the wine daily and try to break up the fruit in the process. When the initial head has subsided strain, transfer to a demijohn and fit an airlock. This wine can be served medium, sweet or, better, as a dessert wine. If it requires extra sugar, this may be added to taste; alternatively, you may feed the wine and develop it as a full dessert. The wine will keep almost indefinitely.

MORELLO CHERRY WINE

8 oz (225 gm) can morello cherries
48 fl oz (1.5 litre) red grape juice
2¼ lb (1.1 kilo) sugar
1 tsp citric acid
wine yeast
water to one gallon (5 litres)

As morello cherries possess a very strong flavour, do not be tempted to use a larger quantity of fruit. If you wish to increase the body of the wine increase the quantity of grape juice used from two bottles to three, reduce the sugar by 6 oz (150 gm) and omit the citric acid. Or you can include the liquid obtained by boiling one pound (0.5 kilo) of bananas and straining — see *Grapefruit and Banana Wine* below.

Place the cherries, syrup and grape juice in a fermenting bucket together with the sugar dissolved in two pints of water and the citric acid. At fermentation temperature add the yeast. Cover, and stir the liquid daily. After three days the stones will have separated from the fruit; remove the stones by decanting the liquid into a second bucket, but allow the fermentation to continue in the presence of the fruit for a further four days. If the stones fail to separate allow fermentation to continue in the presence of the fruit for seven days.

Strain the liquid, squeezing the muslin very gently. Transfer to a demijohn and fit an airlock. Finish in the usual way. The wine may be sweetened to taste with lactose. It is ready for drinking after three to four months and will keep for at least two years. It is ideal for blending with red dry table wines.

GRAPEFRUIT AND BANANA WINE

16 oz (0.5 kilo) can grapefruit segments
2 lb (1 kilo) very ripe bananas
½ cup cold tea
½-1 tsp citric acid
2½ lb (1.25 kilo) sugar
wine yeast
water to 1 gallon

The bananas should be as ripe as possible, with the skins just turning black. Peel and discard the skins. Place the fruit in the saucepan and mash. Add 1½-2 pints (0.75-1 litre) of water and bring just to the boil, stirring to make sure that it does not stick to the base of the pan. Strain the greyish-white liquid into the bucket and discard the fruit pulp. Add the grapefruit segments and syrup, crushing the solid pieces to ensure a more effective extraction. Dissolve the sugar in a pint and a half of hot water. Add the cold tea. The quantity of extra acid that you add will depend upon how acidic you like your wine. Pectic enzyme is not required in this recipe. At 65°-70° F (18.5°-21° C) add the yeast. Stir daily continuing the process of breaking up the fruit. After the initial head has subsided, strain and transfer to a demijohn, topping up if necessary. Finish in the usual manner.

LYCHEE WINE

8 oz (225 gm) can lychees
8 oz (225 gm) can gooseberries
48 fl oz (1.5 litre) white grape juice
1½ lb (0.75 kilo) sugar
pectic enzyme
wine yeast
water to 1 gallon (5 litres)

Mash the fruit and place the purée and the syrup in a bucket, pour in the white grape juice, dissolve the sugar in a pint of water and add to the other ingredients. Add tap water to make the total up to one gallon. At 65°-70° F (18.5°-21° C) add the yeast and provide the enzyme. After seven days strain the mixture, transfer to a demijohn and fit an airlock. The wine may be either drunk dry or medium and will require one or two rackings.

PEACH AND PINEAPPLE WINE

16 oz (0.5 kilo) can peaches
2 pints (1 litre) pineapple juice
1½ lb (0.75 kilo) sugar
½ cup cold tea
1 tsp citric acid
pectic enzyme
wine yeast
water to 1 gallon

Dissolve the sugar in two pints of very hot water; add this to the peaches which should be mashed, the syrup and the pineapple juice. Add the extra acid and cold tea before making the total volume up to one gallon. At 65°-70° F (18.5°-21 C) add the yeast. Stir daily. After seven days filter and transfer to the demijohn, topping up if necessary. Ferment to dryness when 1-2 ounces (25-50 gm) of lactose (to taste) may be added. For the most delicate flavour, drink the wine while it is still young.

In Conclusion

One of the questions that I am constantly being asked is "How do you arrive at the recipes?" I hope that the answer will enable you to improve your wines.

The first stage in the preparation of a wine recipe is the basic idea. The proposed wine is then made. Often the particular wine is disappointing in one or more respects and so the wine is blended with others with a view to eliminating the problems. All blending must be carefully carried out, with exact measurements taken at every stage. The formula for the initial brew is then calculated from everything in the finished wine and a must is then compounded consisting of all the ingredients in their correct proportions. This wine is then made and sampled; if the drink is acceptable then the recipe is quoted. If it is not acceptable then it is back to the blending table!

As your cellar grows then you also will be in a posiion to blend your wines until you achieve the taste you desire. Many expert winemakers are happy to make all their wines by the final blending technique, while others prefer to use the information gleaned from blending as a basis for freshly compounded musts. There is nothing to fear in blending, nor should you feel that you need any special skills. If you are new to winedrinking you may make mistakes, but you will be tasting wine, educating your palate and moving towards a greater understanding of your wine. Do not worry if you do not agree with other people's ideas as to what constitutes a good wine. Wine drinking is subjective at best, with general agreement in only a few areas; home winemaking is still in its infancy and general views are still being formed. Make your own opinions while educating your palate. Wine education is a pleasure; I have studied several subjects throughout my life, but wine is the only one I have found worthy of a lifelong studentship.

BLENDING

To blend a wine first take a full glass, drink it slowly and make mental notes of the wine's faults and good points. Your first method of adjusting the wine should be by following the methods outlined in 'Improving Kit Wines'. After such improvements decide whether you wish to adjust the flavour, body, acidity, tannin, alcohol or sweetness level. You may adjust the level of more than one of the main factors used in winemaking, but do not try to improve more than one characteristic at a time.

Select a wine that is high in the characteristic which you are seeking to emphasise. Measure out 10 ml of the wine into six different glasses and then place 5 ml, 10 ml, 15 ml, 20 ml, 25 ml and 30 ml of the second wine into the glass. Pour a sample of the original wine into a seventh glass. Then taste each of the six glasses in turn, tasting the original wine after each sampling; note which of the wines show an actual improvement. Now, with just the improved wines to hand, sample each until you reach the one that seems best. When tasting wines in this manner it is essential that you take sufficient time between each sample. The palate soon becomes jaded and you should not subject it to much tasting in too short a period of time. Once you have obtained the ideal blend of these two wines you may use another wine to blend in a second characteristic. Because of the decreasing powers of the palate a second blending exercise cannot be performed until the next day. In this way you will soon obtain the formula for your ideal wine.

As a result of the blending process you will have a quantity of wine left over. Combine all the remnants and use as the basis for another blending operation. Where a wine has a high acid or tannin level add this to those low in these charateristics. There is no way in which high levels can be reduced except by using them as a second component in a blend.

After blending a wine it is best to allow the wine to settle for a few days, during which time the component wines will marry. On standing, the chemical components of a wine will interact; in the majority of instances this will result in overall improvements. Occasionally a perfectly clear mixture of two or three wines will throw a sediment or haze. Such imperfections usually clear after a few days, however; failing this wine finings may be added. Wines which contain unfermented sugar often start refermenting if blended with a dry wine. The combined effect of diluting the sugar and the air which inevitably enters the wine during blending reactivates any live yeast cells unless both wines have been chemically treated. So, if you are blending sweet wines it is advisable to store them for about a month under an airlock.

There are few problems with blending providing that you do not use a wine which has any infection, if it does, then the bad wine will spread the germs to the good wine. Wines that do not respond to the suggested treatments must be destroyed. Do not blend a wine that is really bad in terms of balance; it will require so much better wine to dilute the effect that it really is not worth treating. Wines that are out of balance, but not infected, are best used in the kitchen for cooking. The only other type of wine that should never be used in blending is your very best wines. Blending is a process by which a good average drink is achieved; if you incorporate one of your best wines it will then acquire only average characteristics.

PLANNING

I have given instructions for making wines in the shortest possible time so that beginners can commence wine drinking as soon as possible and established winemakers may build up their stocks. Do not rely entirely on this type of wine, however. Plan your winemaking ahead so that you know how much you are going to need in a year's time and aim to have sufficient mature wine ready. To achieve this continuity it is advisable to make five gallons of red and the same quantity of white, thus freeing your equipment for those wines that you require in far smaller quantities. The practice of drinking wines early is less critical now than it was when bottles were laid down for several years. Store your wine in any convenient space but ensure that it is away from extremes of temperature. You should not keep it near hot radiators or in garages, where it may freeze in the winter. Extremes of heat or cold will affect the delicate chemistry being performed inside the bottle.

SERVING WINES

A mystique has developed around the serving of wine and while the direction in which a bottle of port is passed is no more than a ritual, most methods of serving are directed towards presenting the wine in its best possible condition. With the increased use of chemicals in winemaking it is becoming important to allow all wines to breathe before they are served. White wines, except the heavy desserts, and rosés, should be placed in the refrigerator for at least two hours before they are drunk. Today there is an increasing tendency to serve red wines slightly chilled, especially those which are pale in colour and are light bodied. Do not attempt to serve a full-bodied red cold, however; rather, open it four to six hours before it is required and allow it to come to room temperature. One of the beliefs that has passed into winelore is that once a bottle

has been opened its contents must be drunk on the same day. Wine stored under air will quickly oxidise, but not within the space of 24 hours; in all probability the wine will keep in the opened bottle for up to one week. Why open only one bottle with a meal? Since homemade wine will keep for a short period two or three bottles may be opened per meal.

Wine is not only delicious but may well have medicinal benefits and will help to relax you. An aperitif will stimulate the appetite, a little wine will aid digestion and a dessert wine suppress any remaining feelings of hunger. For the vast majority of us the only way that we could hope to enjoy wine to the full is to make it. Unfortunately, country wines are not designed principally for the table and so it is advisable to turn to modern winemaking. Once you have embarked on this most interesting of pastimes you may wish to understand more about wine, its method of preparation, the origins of the great wines and winelore, or you may be happy just to sit back and enjoy the juice of the grape!

Do's and Don'ts

Do ensure that *all* equipment is clean and sterilised.

Do try to maintain a temperature of 65°-70° F (18.5°-21° C) throughout fermentation.

Do check regularly that the airlock contains moisture.

Do ensure that any fruit is liquidised, steam extacted or thoroughly mashed.

Do stir the liquid or agitate the container daily during the initial fermentation.

Do use gelatine or a proprietary fining agent if the wine does not clear within six months.

Do follow manufacturers' instructions carefully when adding chemicals.

Do try as many different brands of grape juice concentrate as possible before deciding which you prefer.

Do blend your wines to improve the quality.

Do taste your wine as frequently as possible and educate your palate.

Don't pour wine straight from the demijohn.

Don't allow wine to stand on a layer of sediment.

Don't allow fermenting or maturing wine to stand at fluctuating temperatures.

Don't allow wine to stand in a demijohn or bottle under air.

Don't use unsterilised corks.

Don't use a diseased wine for blending.

Don't transfer the liquid from the bucket to the demijohn until there is no danger of it spilling over.

Don't forget to check 24-48 hours after the yeast has been added that the wine is working.

Don't bottle until fermentation is complete (except with sparkling wines).

Don't store wine for prolonged periods in plastic containers.

Don't over indulge in wine.

Glossary

ACETALDEHYDE Oxidation product of wine, responsible for some of the character of sherries.

ACETIC ACID The harsh component of vinegar. Any wine possessing this characteristic will be undrinkable.

ACETIFICATION The process by which a wine is turned into vinegar.

ACID Class of chemicals, many of which are corrosive and poisonous. Certain edible varieties are required in a wine in the correct amount to maintain the balance. Wines lacking acid are bland while those with too much are harsh.

AEROBIC FERMENTATION *see* Initial Fermentation.

ALCOHOL Component of the wine responsible for its intoxicating effects. The alcohol in wine is ethanol (ethyl alcohol).

AMYLASE An enzyme added to root vegetables and fruits. Rich in starch it stops haze formation.

ANAEROBIC FERMENTATION *See* Secondary Fermentation.

APERITIF A wine for drinking before a meal to stimulate the appetite. Vermouths and Sherries are amongst the best known commercial aperitifs.

ASTRINGENT Harshness caused by high acid or tannin.

BALANCE When the various components of a wine are present in the correct proportions to complement each other.

BEAD Bubbles of carbon dioxide that travel up through the liquid in sparkling wine.

BENTONITE A naturally occurring clay used to clear wines.

BODY The weight or thickness of a wine. Lack of it results in a thin wine.

BOUQUET	The aroma of the wine.
BRILLIANCE	Describes the highest degree of clarity.
CAMPDEN TABLETS	Sterilising and reducing agent, mainly sodium metabisulphite.
CARBON DIOXIDE	A gas consisting of one part carbon and two parts oxygen released during fermentation.
CHARACTER	Distinctive to a special style of wine.
CAPITALISATION	Addition of sugar to grape juice to supplement that naturally present.
CITRIC ACID	Acid found in citrus fruits. Slightly harsh, it is ideal for winemaking as it forms esters and matures rapidly.
CLARITY	The absence or presence of suspended solids.
CLOUDINESS	Suspension of insoluble particles in the liquid.
DECANTING	Pouring clear wine to separate it from the sediment formed during maturation.
DEMIJOHN	Fermenting vessel.
DESSERT WINE	The fullest and sweetest of all wines, drunk at the end of a meal.
ESTERS	Combination of alcohol and acid, responsible for much of the taste and bouquet of a wine.
ENZYMES	Proteins which bring about specific chemical changes — important to winemakers to break down hazes. Yeast produces natural enzymes that convert sugar to alcohol.
FAREWELL	The taste lingering in the mouth after the wine has been drunk.
FERMENTING TO DRYNESS	The conversion of all available sugar into alcohol.
FILTRATION	Physical separation of suspended particles to aid clarification.
FINING	Chemical treatment of a wine to aid clarification.
GERANIUM FLAVOUR	Off flavour similar to that of the plant, formed as a result of treating a wine with potassium sorbate without the addition of a Campden tablet.
GLYCERINE (GLYCEROL)	Compound responsible for much of the natural body of a wine. Can be added artificially in small amounts (generally not more than 1 tablespoonful per bottle) to any wine.
GOLDEN	Colour of a wine. Golden wines show no sign of browning as a result of oxidation.

GREEN	Used to describe young wine which possess a sharp taste due to it immaturity.
HARSH	a wine containing too much acid or tannin.
HAZE	The presence of minute particles, usually due to starch or pectin that cannot be removed easily.
INITIAL FERMENTATION	The early stage in the yeast's cycle, when it requires air for breeding. It is noticeable by the presence of a vigorous head.
LACTIC ACID	The mellowest of all acids, derived from milk.
LACTOSE	Sugar derived from milk, far less sweet than sucrose.
LEES	Sediment of dead yeast and fruit cells formed during fermentation.
MADERISATION	The development of a caramel flavour, similar to that found in Madeira wines. Can be achieved by using controlled quantities of demerara sugar.
MALOLACTIC FERMENTATION	Occasionally occurring third stage of fermentation, converting malic into lactic acid, which results in a mellowing of the wine.
MATURATION	The ageing of the wine and the chemical changes that accompany the process.
MOUSINESS	A bouquet and flavour reminiscent of mice, due to poor hygiene.
MUST	The liquid and fruit from which the wine is made.
MUSTINESS	Mouldy taste due to leaving the wine too long on the lees.
NUTRIENTS	Compounds other than sugar and acids essential to the yeast development.
OXIDATION	Any chemical process in which compounds react with the oxygen in the air.
PECTIC ENZYME	Sold under a variety of names, it is an enzyme that destroys pectin which would otherwise form a haze.
PECTIN	A carbohydrate found in fruit, especially after prolonged heating.
PROOF	An old standard, still used for spirits, for quoting the alcohol strength of wines. 100^0 is equal to 57.1% alcohol.
RACKING	The separation of the wine from the lees by syphoning.
REDUCTION	Any process by which oxygen is lost from a compound; the reverse of oxidation.

REDUCING AGENT	Any compound that brings about reduction. Sulphur dioxide is the most useful for winemakers.
ROSÉ	A delicate table wine with a pale pink colour.
SECONDARY FERMENTATION	Fermentation conducted in the absence of air (anaerobic). Maximum conversion of sugar to alcohol occurs at this stage.
SOCIAL WINES	Wines for general drinking rather than accompanying a meal; midway between a dessert and table wine in character.
SODIUM METABISULPHITE	Main component of Campden tablets; liberates sulphur dioxide.
STARCH	Non-fermentable carbohydrate; causes haze unless removed by amylase.
STARCH ENZYME	*See* Amylase.
STERILISATION	The killing of micro-organisms.
STUCK FERMENT	Premature cessation of fermentation.
SUCROSE	Chemical name for granulated (household) sugar.
SULPHITE	Used in winemaking to denote the smell and taste of sulphur dioxide.
SULPHUR DIOXIDE	A gas which, when concentrated, has a choking smell. It consists of one unit of sulphur and two units of oxygen.
TABLE WINE	The lightest of all wines designed to be drunk with meals. Table wines should contain about 12% alcohol.
TANNIN	Compound found in the skins and stems of fruit and vegetables. The taste is detected on the gums. An excess of tannin renders a wine harsh; too little tannin yields a bland wine. Tannin is thought to aid clarification.
TARTARIC ACID	The main acid of the grape.
TAWNY WINE	Rich brown-coloured dessert wine. This colour is a fault in lighter wines, whose balance cannot carry the oxidation necessary to produce this effect.
THIN	A wine lacking body.
VINEGAR	A wine in which some of the alcohol has been converted by micro-organisms into acetic acid.
VINOSITY	Wine-like character of the liquid.
YEAST	A fungi which extracts its energy from sugar, yeidling alcohol as a waste product.

Index